D1479145

ATTACKER
The Hudson and Its Flyers

ATTACKER

The Hudson and its Flyers

Geoffrey P. Jones

WILLIAM KIMBER · LONDON

First published in 1980 by
WILLIAM KIMBER & CO. LIMITED
Godolphin House, 22a Queen Anne's Gate,
London, SW1H 9AE

ISBN 0 7183 0237 0

Typeset by Watford Typesetters Ltd.
and printed and bound in Great Britain
by Redwood Burn Limited, Trowbridge and Esher

Contents

List of Illustrations

LIST OF MAPS

COPYRIGHT ACKNOWLEDGEMENTS

Imperial War Museum 25 (both), 27 (both), 28 (bottom), 36, 45, 50, 73, 96 (top), 112 (bottom), 134, 135 (top), 182, 208, 215 (both); Lockheed Corporation 16 (both), 19 (bottom), 97 (bottom), 124 (both), 125 (both), 127; RAAF 80, 82 (both), 85 (both), 87 (both); RCAF 19 (top), 41, 56 (both), 59 (both), 92 (top), 120, 142 top); Other photographs have kindly been provided by A. Arculus, R. Benwell, L. Curtis, R. Feltz, R. Holsgrove, R. C. Jones, L. Montgomery, I. Patterson, C. Shores, F. F. Smith and G. Zwanenburg. The remainder are from the author's collection.

Acknowledgements

This book has taken me some years to write so the list of helpers is naturally long. Fellow authors Lettice Curtis, Ludovic Kennedy, Chris Shores and Jak P. Mallmann Showell were kind enough to assist. In particular I am grateful for permission to quote from *Sub-Lieutenant* by Ludovic Kennedy (B. T. Batsford Ltd. 1942). Roy Benwell, Len Greenham and Bernard Johnson were able to put me in touch with friends who were able to provide information. Leslie Montgomery helped with 'Moon Squadron' information. Welshman Richard Roberts and his friend Gerry Spring provided good contemporary background for 'Desert Squadron' and Gerry Zwanenburg helped with Dutch matters. My brother Ted in Perth, Western Australia again drew the maps. The RAAF in Canberra and the US Navy Department in Washington both answered questions and provided information in their efficient and friendly manner and Peter Robertson in Ottawa put in a great deal of work in selecting RCAF photographs. Crown copyright material is published by permission of the Controller of H.M. Stationery Office.

Lastly I have to thank that friendly person, Arthur Arculus, who alphabetically and in assistance should top the list. This Englishman, now living in New Zealand, has allowed me to make use of the unpublished manuscript he compiled after years of research into the loss of Jim Pedersen. Incorporated in his research was also the story of Bill Tacon and some of that of Ian Patterson. For the use of this information I am truly grateful. His object was to let the relatives, friends and colleagues of Jim Pedersen know of the contribution he made to the air war.

To all those mentioned above, many unnamed contributors and the Lockheed Corporation who designed and built the aircraft, I give my humble thanks for their help and for the enjoyment the writing of the Hudson story has given me.

Abbey Wood 1980

Introduction

The Hudson, an adaptation of the Lockheed B14 civil air liner, was the first American aircraft to go into squadron service with the RAF. When first introduced the Hudson was regarded with some suspicion. It was, flyers said, a dangerous aircraft and could be entrusted only to pilots who had flown thousands of hours and who did not mind being the centre of an occasional bonfire. Gradually this prejudice, which may have had more than a touch of British insularity about it, was overcome. Hudsons fought with fighters, bombed, depth-charged, ferried, observed meteorologically, parachuted, patrolled, photographed, rescued and trained. On every front from Africa to Australia, Canada to China and Iceland to Ireland, Hudsons were to the fore.

In all there were six Marks of Hudsons, the first three with Wright Cyclone engines, and the others with Pratt & Whitney Twin Wasps. Although pilots seem to have preferred the Mark III as an aircraft to fly, the various types showed a general improvement. The main additions were the provision of self-sealing fuel tanks, fully feathering airscrews, side and belly guns. The Hudson's bomb-load was decidedly low, but this was somewhat offset by the large gun armament. The turret, in particular, had a really good field of fire.

The high average of serviceability and the very large number of flying hours which the squadrons were able to keep up month after month were an eloquent tribute to their aircraft. Ground crews and maintenance personnel grew very fond of their charges and took pride in keeping up their reputation for reliability.

The Hudson was one of only a handful of twin-engined aircraft that were in squadron service from the first to the last day of the war in Europe. Squadrons from Great Britain, Australia, Canada, Holland, the United States and other countries, were at various times equipped with Hudsons.

I started my flirtation with the Hudson as a wartime ATC cadet. Whenever aircraft recognition classes were held the one aircraft that was never wrongly identified was the Hudson, so distinctive were the lines. The courtship continued, for when researching an earlier book, I found the Lockheed aircraft kept coming into events. It was then I decided to write about the ubiquitous Hudson. I thought then, and am certain now, that the part the aircraft played in the battle against the Axis deserves to be recorded.

I managed to cadge some wartime trips from Yeovilton and Exeter airfields and it was from the latter that nine white painted Hudsons, from No 608 Squadron, flew to Gibraltar for Operation Torch, the invasion of North Africa, in October 1942.

Writing this book has given me very real pleasure; my only concern is that I may not have done the aircraft full justice. I decided against writing a 'nuts and bolts' history of the Hudson and have not burdened the reader with technical details, but presented an anthology of the Hudson's achievements in its different roles. I fully realise that I have omitted stories of training, and have indeed not mentioned at all some squadrons that were equipped with Hudsons, but, as most aircrew knew, much of their time consisted of routine tasks and boredom; the actions reproduced in this book probably occupied less than one per cent of a pilot's career, and even describing similar actions can appear repetitious and therefore boring to the reader. I have therefore given representative cameos.

Some of the events have been described before, but in each case I believe I have included something new and previously unpublished. The photographs created something of a problem, but finally I secured enough from all over the world to make the book truly representative. I would have liked to present more pictures from the Home Front, but the difficulty was that unofficial photography was prohibited in Britain during the early war years when the Hudson was most active.

I have recorded part of the story of the Hudson. Other enthusiasts have done better for there are Hudsons preserved in collections in Australia, Britain and the United States for a new generation of aircraft buffs to see the model that helped defeat the foe.

ATTACKER
The Hudson and Its Flyers

I

In the Beginning

Early in 1938 the Air Ministry were having a long hard look at the composition of the Royal Air Force aircraft in the circumstances of a probable European war involving Britain. Spitfires and Hurricanes were of more than adequate quality as the fighter strength; Hampdens, Whitleys and Wellingtons composed the bombing force, and the Blenheim and Anson combined the reconnaissance role.

It was thought that the reconnaissance strength should be increased and a new single-engine monoplane trainer should be ordered if available. With these objectives in mind a Purchasing Commission was sent to America in April. One of the Commission members was Air Commodore A. T. Harris, later to be famous as the Commander-in-Chief of Bomber Command. Bert Harris, as he was known, had recently been designated as Air Officer Commanding in Palestine and was about to take up the position when given this new assignment. The other members of the Commission were an industrial expert, a civil servant and technician, with Squadron Leader Horrex as test pilot.

A visit to the Lockheed Corporation works at Burbank California resulted in orders for the Lockheed Model 214, later named Hudson. A visit to the North American plant in California convinced the Commission that the Harvard would serve as the trainer, and it too was ordered.

The Hudson was a military version of the Lockheed 14, an eleven-seat passenger aircraft, sometimes known as the Electra. Air Commodore Harris was much impressed with the aircraft which he thought highly suitable for reconnaissance work; and he also thought the executives running the factory knew their business inside out, despite their comparative youth.

On arrival at the factory a mock-up fuselage awaited their inspection. In this version there was a tunnel passageway under the two pilots' seats purporting to give access to the front gun position. This was impracticable. The navigator was positioned behind the pilot's

The first Hudsons arrived as deck cargo. Shown here are two already aboard and four more waiting to be hoisted aboard the ship at Los Angeles en-route to Liverpool in 1939.

Final check in California before transfer abroad.

seat with no view worth mentioning in any direction.

The Lockheed executives were however extremely receptive and appreciative of ideas and advice. After a discussion of the short-comings, for British purposes, of the military aircraft as shown in the mock-up, it was decided that the essential improvements could only be made by redesigning the whole forward layout on a one-pilot-plus-automatic-control basis.

Air Commodore Harris was asked to come back in a few days to see a new mock-up, but he told the Lockheed executives he would not be able to do this as he had to visit other aircraft factories. It was therefore a surprise when only a day later Lockheeds' sent a car to take him to the works to see a mock-up containing all the asked for requirements. The mock-up was in plywood, fitted complete in every detail, with two alternative noses hinged on to a real aircraft all ready for inspection.

In both the layouts the pilot was to port, the wireless operator immediately behind him. A practical passageway to starboard led past the pilot to the navigator's position forward. This layout gave ample room and adequate personal communication between the pilot and the navigator, front-gunner and bomb-aimer. For look-out and fighting purposes both a navigator and a front turret gunner could if necessary be comfortably accommodated forward of the pilot's position.

The two alternative arrangements offered respectively two fixed guns firing forward controlled by the pilot, with a large navigator/bomb-aimer/look-out position forward of the pilot, or a front turret position with a navigator's position between the front turret and the pilot as outlined above. It was the former that was ordered for use with the RAF even though the Commission thought the aircraft over large for fixed guns.

The mock-ups clinched the deal. Air Commodore Harris was convinced that anyone who could produce a mock-up in a day would certainly make good their promises; Lockheed's certainly did when they secured the order.

Squadron Leader Horrex reported on the flight characteristics and the Commission were able to signal to Britain :

Fitted with a suitable British turret fore and aft and with a tunnel gun position (or if necessary a retracting bottom turret, in the after cabin) this aircraft, with the redesigned forward part of fuselage as shown in the mock-up to us, should prove not only an excellent general reconnaissance aircraft but a formidable medium bomber of high performance. The cabin space aft makes it, further, a useful troop carrier-general purposes types should such a need later arise.

Space and available lift are ample for a much greater range and/or bomb load than those asked for purely reconnaissance purposes. The removable extra range tank and the complete rails and strong points for the maximum bomb loads (in tier, horizontally) were left in the specification in case of future need and because no ponderable gain in performance or saving in cost seemed likely to result from their removal.

It must be borne in mind that this aircraft, as a single pilot job, is only suited to the tasks intended for it on the assumption that the automatic pilot forms a basic part of the specification. The American Sperry pilot seems to work well and reliably.

The turret and armament fittings would leave off at the strong points necessary to enable our own gear to be added. Intercommunication would be supplied and fitted by the manufacturer. Radio could be ordered complete if found suitable, or alternatively the necessary bondings. Wireless operation space, seat, table and antennae could be built in while leaving only the sets to be provided by us.

It was agreed that Boulton Paul would provide the power-operated dorsal turret, with two .303 Browning machine-guns, when the aircraft arrived in England.

The first Hudson flew from Burbank in December 1938. In the meantime however, the British Prime Minister Neville Chamberlain, had flown to Germany to meet Adolf Hitler at his home. The aircraft selected for the flight was the new Lockheed 14 belonging to British Airways. The aircraft flew from Heston on 15 September and returned from Cologne nine days later. The Germans therefore had time to look at the civil version of the military aircraft that the British had just ordered from America in large numbers.

The first Hudsons started arriving in Britain in the early spring of 1939 by ship, as deck cargo. On arrival they were reassembled, fitted out as necessary – gun-turrets were added and the very first one ready for use was delivered to Coastal Command in May 1939.

Much later Lettice Curtis, the ATA pilot was to record :

Hudson 1 of No 13 Squadron RCAF with unusual roundel markings in November 1940.

A wet day in sunny California as these Hudson V's have the final touch applied.

ATA pilot Faith Newmark signs the Form 700 before accepting a Hudson.

The Hudson was never one of my favourite aircraft. It was what
we called a swinger, meaning that it had a marked tendency to
swing during the landing run. We were expected, as with other
types of aircraft, to three-point them, that is, to touch down on
landing with main and tail wheels at the same time. This involved
a marked change of attitude during the 'flare out' which reduced
the effectiveness of the rudder during the landing run. The other

thing that took a bit of getting used to was the brakes which were operated by pulling a car-type ratchet lever, set in the central pedestal to the right of the pilot's seat. In order to produce differential breaking through rudder bar movements one had theoretically to set the lever a couple of notches out but in fact, the correct setting was difficult to find. Thus, if braking became necessary during the landing run, one had to lean to one side and pull, making sure that at the same time the rudder bar was correctly operated. Often during this manoeuvre differential brake was unwittingly applied and it was not an uncommon sight to see a Hudson ending its landing run with a ground loop; luckily the undercarriage was robust and the pilot in most cases got away with it. This was just as well because the fuel tanks were directly above the undercarriage struts and a heavy landing or broken undercarriage led very easily to ruptured fuel tanks and fire. Like everything else pilots who flew Hudsons consistently got used to them and liked them well enough. As they only seemed to come my way about once in six months I never really got used to them and in consequence, always had slight misgivings about the landing when I found myself with a chit for one to ferry.

The first squadron to receive the Hudson was No 224, who until this time had been flying Ansons. It was soon found that the Hudson was a better all-round aircraft than the Anson, and indeed its impressive performance was only a little less than that of the Blenheim in speed, but had a greater load capacity and comparatively more cabin room.

The crew found their positions in the Hudson extremely comfortable, a decided advantage when long and tedious patrols formed a large part of operations. The well-upholstered seats and a good heating and ventilation system made the American-built aircraft immediately popular with the crews. Within a short time the Hudson replaced the Anson and the latter was relegated to the training and communication duties that had one time been envisaged for the Hudson.

By the outbreak of war in September, crews of 224 Squadron based at Leuchars were already well practised in their new aircraft for the struggle that lay ahead – a struggle in which the Hudson was to play a very vital role as a scourge to both the Germans and Japanese.

II

Coastal Command

Coastal Command was responsible for all air escorts for convoys and anti-submarine patrols round the British Isles by shore-based aircraft. During the first few months of the war the work of Coastal Command proved more strenuous than that carried out by the other commands, since a large-scale German air offensive had not then been launched, whereas submarine and mine warfare on British and neutral shipping began the hour war broke out.

Two days before the outbreak of war Hudsons became operational. They then began to come across the Atlantic in a steady flow, until by the autumn of 1941, eleven Hudson squadrons were operational in Coastal Command; this was the greatest number at any one time.

The area of sea kept under survey by aircraft of Coastal Command was much larger than generally realised; it stretched from the Arctic Circle to Africa, from the western coasts of Europe to some hundreds of miles west, north-west and south-west of Ireland, and in the east from the northern tip of Norway along the European coastline to the Pyrenees.

Until the convoy system came into force the Command maintained an almost continual patrol over the Western Approaches to Great Britain. The task of the air escort was not only to protect the convoy against attacks by enemy aircraft, submarines and surface craft but to look for mines and to round up ships which may have straggled from the convoy. Another task of Coastal Command was to provide escorts for the fishing fleets in the North Sea and in the Irish Sea. The Navy dubbed aircraft on this duty 'Kipper Kites'.

The early days of the war, so boring to so many, were full of activity for the Hudsons. Constant patrols, reconnaissances and escorts were flown over the North Sea, and a very large number of the early air skirmishes were fought by Hudsons. Their opponents were usually Dornier flying boats and Heinkel 111's but there were also occasional brushes with Messerschmitt Bf 109's.

Typical of the patrols of this time is one by a pilot operating with

No 224 Squadron out of Leuchars. The Hudson limped back with twenty bullet holes and oil pouring from its port engine, which was out of commission. In spite of this the pilot landed the machine safely. The crew consisting of a pilot, navigator, wireless operator and an air-gunner had an average age of just over twenty, all returned uninjured.

The pilot said:

We left the aerodrome about noon on a normal patrol. About 160 miles over the North Sea I spotted two planes and turned to the navigator and told him, 'I think these are Germans!'

We speeded after the planes. They saw us and tried to get away, but we followed. I climbed into the sun and attacked one of the planes, leaving the other to clear off. We kept on the enemy's tail for a considerable time. He dodged this way and that, but I climbed into the sun and managed to swoop down on him without his seeing us. I saw the rear gunner, a fair-haired man, in the German plane, slumped over his turret. I judged that he was shot.

The gunner who occupied the rear turret then took up the story.

We overshot the German several times, and I could fire right into the heart of the machine. At times I could almost have touched it. I could even see the bullet holes with which it was riddled. The German did his utmost to escape, but my pilot swooped up and down and clung to him like a terrier.

Sometimes we were only about fifty feet above the sea during the flight. We made six attacks on the German before we were hit ourselves. The bullets from the German seemed to shower around me, but I did not know there was any serious damage until the port motor cracked up. A bullet from the Dornier's cannon struck the oil pressure tank and the motor suddenly went dead.

The last I saw of the German he was gliding down towards the sea and if he managed to get home he was lucky.

After the fight the British wireless operator had to radio for directions to bring the aircraft back to the East Scottish aerodrome. He said: 'All I could do was to sit by my apparatus and wait for the outcome. When the port engine gave out I wired for directions and we landed at Leuchars practically blind.'

As with so many attacks at this time, the result was inconclusive and only an 'aircraft damaged' could be claimed.

From these battles the Luftwaffe gained considerable respect for the aggressiveness of the Hudson's pilots and the capabilities of their aircraft. One Dornier lasted just 35 seconds against a Hudson's guns, and on another occasion eight Me109's were insufficient to dispose of a Hudson which returned home safely in spite of being seriously damaged.

The next two squadrons to be operational with Hudsons were No 233, also out of Leuchars, and No 220 at Thornaby-on-Tees. On 1 November 1939 His Majesty King George VI, Chief of the Air Staff Sir Cyril Newall, the Air Officer Commanding Coastal Command Sir Frederick Bowhill and other dignitaries visited Thornaby where His Majesty inspected the operations room, looked over a Hudson then inspected the crews on parade. Nine days later two Hudsons from the squadron damaged a Do18 flying boat which broke up on alighting in the sea.

On 29 November New Zealander Edward W. Tacon, serving with No 233 Squadron, on patrol to Lister Light, surprised a Do18 on the water and sank it with his Hudson's front guns. Bill Tacon was to be closely associated with the Hudson throughout its span of operations, frequently as a mast-height attacker; he was still flying the aircraft six years later and clocked up a total of over 1,800 hours on Hudsons and probably spent more time piloting the versatile warplane than anybody else.

The fourth squadron to re-equip with Hudsons was No 206 operating out of Bircham Newton in Norfolk. Many warships and convoys owed their survival to the activities of East Coast Hudsons. It was at this time also that there began the intimate and unfriendly association between the Hudson and the German battle-cruisers *Scharnhorst* and *Gneisenau*, which were shadowed, bombed and blockaded until their escape in bad weather from Brest two years later.

The opening of the campaign in Norway in April 1940 brought more work for the Hudsons. The coastline was ceaselessly patrolled, and the bombing trip to Stavanger became a routine run. The versatility of the Hudson was beginning to be appreciated.

One of the Hudsons over Stavanger on 17 April was No 233 Squadron's N7325, flown by Bill Tacon with three crew and a naval

(*Above*) Kondor shot down by Hudson within sight of a convoy on 23 July 1940. Four of the crew are in the water hanging on to their dinghy which is just inflating. (*Right*) Dornier flying boat brought down by a Hudson after a 35 second engagement off Norway.

observer. The latter was being carried because HMS *Suffolk* was bombarding Stavanger and he was spotting and communicating the results to the County Class cruiser below. Another new role for the versatile aircraft.

A few days later while flying another Hudson in a battle flight escorting French destroyers Bill Tacon's Hudson was attacked by two Me109's, hit three times and had to land at Lossiemouth.

Early the next month the New Zealander was carrying out a meteorological reconnaissance off the Norwegian coast when the air-craft was machine-gunned by German troopships off Stavanger. Later that same day HMS *Kelly* leading the Fifth Destroyer Flotilla was torpedoed and her sea escorts required air assistance. Bill Tacon was one of the Hudson pilots sent to cover the stricken destroyer; un-fortunately but understandably the Hudsons were fired on by a trigger-happy gunner aboard one of the destroyers but no damage was reported. The next day nine Hudsons from No 220 Squadron escorted the famous destroyer which was now being towed. The last flight of three aircraft chased three Heinkels which had tried to bomb but were outdistanced and returned to the destroyers. Jim Pedersen, a New Zealander with the squadron, recorded in his log book: 'High level bombing by enemy aircraft – no hits!'

A week later Bill Tacon was flying his Hudson at 100 feet up the Elbe to bomb oil tanks at Hamburg. The aircraft was hit many times by shells with the result that the wireless operator was wounded in the arm. 'Never again' recorded the New Zealand pilot.

After the invasion of the low countries and the epic of Dunkirk, the Hudson crews found they were filling in their time with bombing missions to the invasion ports, factories and installations on the long enemy coastline, as well as with their everlasting patrols and they later worked up to the great anti-shipping offensive. To ease the strain on their overworked railways the Germans introduced coastal convoys between ports in Norway, Denmark, Holland, Belgium and France. This long line of communication was clearly asking to be hit – the Hudsons hit it. In company with other aircraft they harried the convoys day and night, at sea and in harbour. Increases in anti-aircraft armament and escort vessels failed to stop the Hudsons coming in from 50 feet to plant their 250-pounders into the sides and decks of the enemy merchantmen. At least one pilot found on the wings of his Hudson some small bits of wood which the Germans had recently been using on one of their ship's masts. Some-

Crossing the coastline at 2,000 feet. This Hudson on a reconnaissance over Norwegian fiords was taking photographs of enemy ships lurking in the waterways.

A Hudson crew inspect a shell hole in the wing, a relic from a Norwegian trip.

This Hudson hit the sea during a night bombing raid in the Bay. The pilot flew it 260 miles back to base in the dark without an ASI and both airscrews damaged. Three bombs were torn out of the bomb bay and the tail unit of a fourth was washed away by the sea while the bomb remained on the rack.

This Hudson while flying low in search of enemy shipping off Norway had a large hole prized in the floor by a projecting rock on a small island.

times losses were severe, but frequently the attackers would all arrive safely back at base – a great tribute not only to the ground and air crews, but also to the Lockheed designers and the workers.

The climax of the Hudson's anti-shipping activities came in the late autumn of 1941 when British, Canadian and Dutch squadrons were responsible for by far the greater part of the destruction, and the brilliant attack on Aalesund, where five ships were hit, two factories set on fire, and a barracks and wireless station bombed, was carried out unaided, by only nine Hudsons.

Meanwhile on the other side of the British Isles a less spectacular but equally vital battle was going on : the Battle of the Atlantic. It was natural for the Hudsons to play their part in this struggle also, and they did so with equal distinction. Instead of comparatively short trips with plenty of excitement, the anti-submarine Hudsons had to undertake long trips over the ocean through very bad weather. In this theatre their great reliability at once won the trust of all who flew in them. Hour after hour their engines would perform faultlessly, whatever the conditions, and the majority of crews never experienced a failure.

Occasionally the Atlantic Hudsons were called upon for anti-aircraft as well as anti-submarine escort duties, and the battle between the Hudson and the Kondor was often fought out. The Kondor too was an adaptation of a civil machine, but apparently Lockheed's was the better of the two.

Their patrols and escorts in the Atlantic took the Hudsons to a wide variety of climates. Iceland, Scotland, the Western Isles, Ireland, Cornwall, Gibraltar, North and West Africa were normal Hudson bases, while in times of stress they operated from the USA and even Greenland. As is usual with this type of work, there are few highlights or epic deeds, but as will shortly be seen it was an important chapter in the story of the Hudson; a chapter which might indeed have been even more exciting had the aircraft been less dependable.

III

The Navy's Here!

When, in 1939, war became imminent German supply ships were allocated their wards; *Altmark* to *Graf Spee* and her sister-ship *Westerwald* to *Deutschland*.

In August, just one month before the outbreak of hostilities, the pocket-battleship *Graf Spee* left Germany to be in position in the Atlantic when war was declared. In the Atlantic she met up with her replenishment ship, *Altmark*, which had left two weeks earlier but in the meantime had filled her tanks with oil in Texas.

At the end of September the battleship received orders from Germany to attack merchantmen. In between forays *Graf Spee* met *Altmark*, which kept herself well hidden off the main shipping routes, refuelled and replenished from the supply-ship and in return off-loaded prisoners that had been captured from the merchant vessels. The two ships met for the last time on 7 December when the pocket-battleship handed over the last of the prisoners from five ships that had been sunk. *Altmark* now had 299 prisoners on board.

Graf Spee sailed west looking for rich pickings off the coast of South America. She found instead the British cruisers *Exeter*, *Ajax* and *Achilles* waiting for her at first light on 13 December. Badly damaged in the action with the cruisers, the German ship asked for, and was given, permission to put into the neutral Uruguayan port of Montevideo. Three days later she sailed out and scuttled herself as she believed she was to be opposed by superior British forces. In the meantime, the prisoners aboard *Graf Spee* who had not been put aboard *Altmark* were released and wasted no time in informing the British Consul about the prison-ship. The First Lord of the Admiralty, at that time Winston Churchill, ordered that the floating prison must be located and the prisoners released.

While the Royal Navy were keeping an eye out for *Altmark*, making sure that the British seamen captives did not reach Germany, the captain of the German ship took her to the South Atlantic for the double purpose of completing necessary repair work on her engines and keeping out of the way while the heat was on.

It was not until 21 January that *Altmark* finally started her journey home after her engines had been tested. The radio officers on the German ship had picked up a description of their ship issued to the Royal Navy. *Altmark* was described as having a large single yellow funnel aft, purporting to be the *Sogne* of Oslo. *Sogne* was quickly erased and replaced by *Haugesund* and this was followed later by *Chirqueue* and the ship was painted grey. *Altmark* successfully avoided contact with enemy forces on her journey north up through the Atlantic as she made her way south of Iceland and north of the Faeroe Islands to make a landfall off the coast of Norway. It was the evening of 13 February when *Altmark*, again reverting to her correct name, arrived in Norwegian territorial waters. It was her captain's intention to steam down to the Skagarrak inside Norwegian territorial waters and then sail across to Germany under cover of darkness. At this time Norway was still neutral.

Two days later, after the night had been spent off Trondheim, *Altmark* was boarded by Norwegian naval officers from a gun-boat. The German captain told the boarding party that his ship was on its way from Texas to Germany and, evidently satisfied the Norwegians left. Later *Altmark* was hailed by a torpedo-boat again and was asked, 'Are there any persons on board who belong to the armed forces of a belligerent country, or any sailors or civilians who were nationals of a belligerent country?' The Norwegians were told that there were no such persons on board. Another Norwegian vessel hailed the prison-ship off Bergen – and it was from this port that the British first learned that their quarry was off the coast of Norway. A submarine with an armed party aboard was despatched to intercept, but failed to locate the German ship.

Early in the morning of 16 February the leader of a Hudson squadron at the Coastal Command airfield at Thornaby-on-Tees had been awoken and ordered to take his aircraft to search off the Norwegian coast for *Altmark* : he was told in the Operations Room that she was a 20,000 ton tanker-type vessel and, when last reported, had a black hull with yellow or white upperworks; the most distinctive feature was her large single funnel aft. He found the ship was not listed in Lloyd's Register of Shipping. The pilot takes up the story himself :

We set off first, for the opposite coast. Visibility was not too good, but our crews had done this journey a number of times since the war began. It later became a beautiful day, with gorgeous sunshine and a Mediterranean sky. Visibility increased to more than ten times. We proceeded to comb thoroughly an area from the extreme south point of Norway northwards. Flying well outside territorial waters, I examined every mile with binoculars.

Then, fifteen miles ahead, I saw a smudge of smoke, and a minute later a ship with a black hull and cream upperworks steaming directly towards us. We swung out slightly to get a broadside view of her. My heart sank when I recognised from her lines that she could not be our quarry.

But fifteen seconds later I spotted something else – a grey ship, with funnel aft – the distinctive feature of *Altmark*. We flew up to her at 1,000 feet and inspected her through glasses at a mile range. Then we turned in on top of her for a close inspection. As we dived my eyes were riveted on the stern, searching for a name. I saw letters about a foot high. Because of the speed at which we were diving the letters seemed to dance in a jumble. I expected that when they could be read they would spell a Norwegian name. I could not suppress a whoop of joy when I saw that they read *Altmark*. Of course, we know now that the Germans had reverted to her own name earlier in the week.

All the members of my crew saw the word *Altmark*. I caught sight of my men out of the corner of my eye. They were not holding one thumb up – the signal of success; each man had both thumbs up!

For a few moments they went wild as we swept across the *Altmark*'s decks at funnel height. I could see only one man on the deck. He was hanging over a rail as if seasick or looking for mines. There was no other sign of life aboard and not the slightest evidence of any alarm. Not a shot was fired from the *Altmark*'s hidden guns.

Below, on the German ship, some of the prisoners heard the aircraft and were able to see the guards and some of the crew and officers of the ship collected on the fore deck, they all had their lifejackets on and bits of their personal effects with them. The internees knew it must be a British aircraft because the Germans would not have bothered to put their lifejackets on for a Norwegian.

It was after mid-day when the leader of the Coastal Command Hudson radioed back to base that the enemy had been sighted. This was just the news the Navy were waiting for and a naval force on patrol made for the reported position. Leading the force was the cruiser *Arethusa* and she was accompanied by some of the Fourth Destroyer Flotilla, commanded by Captain Vian in *Cossack*.

Cossack moved to head off the *Altmark*, but the German ship slipped into nearby Jossing Fiord at the very south of Norway where she was spotted by a Hudson from No 233 Squadron. The two Norwegian gunboats which had escorted the German prison ship down the coast were still with her. The captain of one of the gunboats came on board *Cossack* and assured Captain Vian that there were no prisoners on board. The British ship withdrew but later, after receiving further orders, steamed into the fiord through the ice.

Passing the protesting Norwegian gunboats *Cossack* crunched her way slowly through the ice and directed her searchlight onto the *Altmark* as by now it was getting dark. As the *Cossack* approached, the *Altmark* lunged astern. The captain of the destroyer swung his ship sideways, but the German ship scraped the full length of the *Cossack*. When the ships were eight feet apart, grappling irons were thrown onto the tanker and the boarding party jumped aboard.

The German captain was forcibly dispossessed of the engine-room telegraphs which resulted in the ship grounding on a rock shelf while making about four knots sternway. There was some hand-to-hand fighting and an occasional shot. Some of the crew jumped overboard on to the ice and escaped; the Germans lost seven killed.

The boarding party opened up a battened-down hatch and shouted: 'Are there any prisoners down there?' With one voice they answered the question. Then came the words that were to make newspaper headlines: 'The Navy's here!'

The 299 prisoners were put aboard the destroyers and rushed back to the Scottish port of Leith, escorted all the way by Hudson aircraft.

In Germany, Norway was seen to be pro-Allied following the *Altmark* incident and a week later Hitler charged his operational planning staff to put in hand plans for the invasion of the country. The seaborne invasion commenced in April 1940 and two sister-ships of *Altmark*, *Dithmarschen* and *Nordmark*, were on hand to replenish the Kriegsmarine ships. The latter ship, previously known as *Wester-wald*, had already completed one operation as supply-ship to the *Deutschland* at the beginning of the war. She was now returning to Germany after an absence of over a hundred days. She left Stavanger in southern Norway on the evening of Friday 19 July, accompanied by some minesweepers, on the last leg of her journey back to Hamburg. Early on the Sunday morning one of the minesweepers *M8*, ahead of the convoy reported sighting a Lockheed aircraft. Another M-boat fired three or four rounds at it as it disappeared westwards.

The Hudson, of No 233 Squadron, had taken off from the airfield at Leuchars Fifeshire at 0320 that morning. At 0615 her crew saw and attacked a small motor vessel. The stick of bombs fell astern, and the Hudson then raked the bridge with machine-gun fire. Although all the bombs had been dropped the Hudson continued on reconnaissance duties and it was half-an-hour later that the minesweepers and the *Nordmark* were spotted. As there was no cloud available and it was quite likely that the ships would call for air assistance, the aircraft did not venture too close. The Hudson completed its patrol and on landing reported seeing an 'oil-tanker' of 10,000 tons escorted by five sloops which had put up slight anti-aircraft fire.

Twenty minutes after the Hudson landed in Scotland, a flight of three Hudsons from No 220 Squadron took off from their Yorkshire base and were directed on to the convoy. The flight had been airborne for two-and-a-quarter hours when they sighted the *Nordmark* escorted by five sloops, one ahead and a pair on either side. Aboard the German ships 'Action Stations' was sounded as soon as the aircraft were seen – an attack had been expected after the morning sighting.

The Hudson pilots decided to attack from different angles, one from ahead on the starboard side, one from ahead on the port side and the other from abeam on the starboard side, directly out of the sun.

There was no preamble. The pilots flew straight into the attack. B-Baker, attacking from ahead, flew across the bow and was immediately fired on from the ship. His first bomb fell less than ten yards from the ship's bow, damaging the hull and causing water to pour in. The second bomb hit the starboard side damaging a tank cover, the gangway, water-pipes and cables, and the derrick. The starboard petrol tank was hit and the cutter on its davits was damaged by splinters, rendering it useless. This bomb put the bridge telegraph and gyro-compass out of action. The third bomb fell forward of the aft pump-room, ripping through a stairway and the main deck. The blast from the bomb tore open the deck and the life-floats were blown out of position and crushed.

U-Uncle came right across the ship from starboard and dropped a bomb which missed the ship by over 350 yards. The Germans thought that this machine then circled round and attacked from the port side ahead, but in fact this was the third aircraft F-Freddie.

F-Freddie made a bow to stern attack and as he came in he was hit by accurate shooting from the *Nordmark* and the tailplane and the port side of the fuselage were damaged. This Hudson dropped two bombs; the first fell over 400 yards from the ship but the second was less than 20 yards from the ship's side and caused further damage to the hull. As the aircraft roared over the ship, the air-gunners let fly and the bullets ripped into the ship injuring five of the crew, one of them badly.

The machine then flew off westwards towards the English coast and home. U-Uncle claimed to have hit the ship with two bombs but it is possible that the hits claimed were in fact caused just previously by B-Baker. F-Freddie claimed a hit on the stern, but his second bomb had fallen just wide and the hit claimed was probably caused by the third bomb of B-Baker.

When the aircraft arrived back at Thornaby at 1450 the crew reported that when they attacked, the smaller ships scattered and the *Nordmark* turned to starboard with large clouds of white smoke issuing from amidships. They had probably not realised that while the attack was on, *Nordmark* had been zig-zagging at high speed to try and give the attacking aircraft a more difficult aiming point.

The Germans did not have much respite, however, as another attack was on the way. Four more Hudsons had taken off from Leuchars, three from No 233 Squadron and the other from No 224 Squadron, also based there. These aircraft set course for the target forty minutes after the first three attacking aircraft and they arrived over the ships half-an-hour after the previous attack had ended, they reported the ships as travelling at fifteen knots. They broke up into two flights of two aircraft each.

Captain Grau ordered 'Action Stations' to be sounded again on the *Nordmark* when the four Hudsons were first seen on the starboard

Nordmark was sighted by a Hudson of No 233 Squadron and the shadow of the attacking aircraft can be seen at the stern of the ship. White smoke can be seen rising from a bomb hit amidships on the port side.

side. This time the first attack came from the stern of the ship on the port side and four bombs were dropped. The pilot claimed three of his bombs overshot, but from *Nordmark* fountains of water were seen erupting in the ship's wake and the crew on the German ship claimed that the bombs were dropped prematurely because the aircraft came under heavy fire. The aircraft, they claimed, had been damaged. The pilot, for his part, thought that one of his bombs had hit the ship amidships as there was smoke issuing from there.

The second aircraft, attacking from the same quarter, was not seen to drop any bombs, although both of the aircraft heavily machine-gunned the guns' crews aft before flying off to the west. The other half of the formation had no chance of attacking as a flight of Me110 fighters appeared and at once engaged the British planes. These twin-engined fighters were no match for a single-engined fighter but were formidable opponents to a twin-engined bomber and one of the Hudsons was seen to crash into the sea in flames after a short fight. On board the *Nordmark* the crew were delighted to see their attackers themselves under attack and cheered as the Hudson hit the sea ablaze.

The aircraft that had led the last raid was indeed hit as the Germans claimed. It was badly hit by fire from the ship in its petrol tanks and the pilot thought he might not have enough petrol to reach home. An aircraft from 224 Squadron was detailed to meet him but he arrived back safely an hour after his ETA with hardly any petrol left in his Hudson's tanks.

The Hudson destroyed by the Me110 was not the only aircraft lost in the attack as one aircraft from both No 224 and No 233 Squadron failed to return. One of the No 233 Squadron Hudsons to survive the raid was flown by New Zealander Bill Tacon. He piloted Hudson N7244, accompanied again by Flying Officer Edwards. Bill modestly recorded in his log book: 'Striking force – bombed tanker – hit in petrol tank by AA – two machines lost.'

Back on the *Nordmark* damage from the attack was being assessed. Most of the damage had been caused by the three bombs dropped by the leading aircraft in the first attack. The first bomb which fell into the water close to the ship's side had made a hole six feet by three through which the sea came in. The damage control party effectively sealed off this part of the ship. The second bomb amidships did the most damage and caused the smoke that was seen by the later attacking aircraft. Below deck all the equipment and material in the top flat was destroyed and nothing could be done until the compartment had been emptied. The third bomb had made a hole a yard across in the upper deck, damaging the steel ladders and gangways and the bulkhead in the after pump room. The fourth bomb, dropped by the third attacking Hudson close to the ship's port side, had damaged the boiler room with splinters.

During the raids the *Nordmark* had expended 800-900 rounds of 2 cm explosive cartridges and 1500-1600 rounds of explosive machine-gun ammunition. It was a dramatic end to a long voyage. When the *Nordmark* arrived back in Hamburg two days later she had steamed over eleven thousand sea miles in the 108 days she had been away from the Fatherland.

Ironically, it was a mixed blessing for the British that *Nordmark* was not sunk in the attack, for later she was at sea in the South Atlantic with the *Admiral Scheer*, where she replenished not only the warship but armed merchant cruisers and U-boats, both German and Italian. Later she served as supply ship for the *Tirpitz* and the *Scharnhorst* in Northern Norway. However, when hostilities ended she was captured in Copenhagen, allocated to the British and joined the Royal Navy as HMS *Bulawayo* until scrapped in a Scottish yard in 1955.

IV

Dunkirk - Where was the RAF?

This was the question asked by many troops who arrived back in England after being rescued from the British Expeditionary Force in 1940. The rescue – covering a period of days and concentrated mainly in the Dunkirk area – by little boats, including those crewed by amateur sailors, is often described as a 'miracle' but the soldiers who were attacked on the beaches by the Luftwaffe were bitter that the Royal Air Force was not more in evidence. But one aircraft was there all the time – the Hudson.

The 'phoney' war ended on 10 May 1940 when, without warning, German troops invaded neutral Belgium and Holland. Immediately the British and French armies were asked to assist these countries which previously would not allow the Allied troops on their soil. The plea came rather too late as the German armoured columns moved relentlessly westwards outflanking the French Maginot Line. German troops quickly reached the River Somme at Abbeville almost on the Channel coast, thus effectively cutting through the Allied defences and leaving only one course open to the British Expeditionary Force, to retreat to the coast, form a defensive perimeter and attempt an evacuation by sea.

Holland surrendered on 14 May, Belgium four days later. In the meantime France carried on fighting. As they retreated the French tried repeatedly to get more fighter assistance from the RAF, but the authorities in England did not want to fight out a war of attrition with the Luftwaffe over French soil. It was obvious that the Battle of Britain would follow the Battle of France.

Air Chief Marshal Sir Hugh Dowding, Commander-in-Chief of Fighter Comamnd, was fearful that the Air Staff would accede to the request of the French Government, backed by Prime Minister Winston Churchill. Some 250 Hurricanes had been lost in the ten days preceding the Belgian surrender and losses on such a scale could not be allowed to continue. When fighting over one's own country it was often possible for machines damaged in combat to reach their home base, be repaired and the plane and pilot continue the fight. For aircraft more seriously damaged, the pilot was often able to bale out and be saved, and in these early days of the war the pilot was equally as valuable as his aircraft. Dowding was keeping his Spitfires back for the Home Defence role but nevertheless both Hurricanes and Spitfires were carrying out two or three sorties a day over the evacuation area. Dowding also considered that the air fighting over the Channel during the Dunkirk evacuation was uneconomical because the fighters were virtually being used as 'overseas' fighters with the resultant risk of loss of both aircraft and pilots. However, had it not been for the constant fighter patrolling far inland on France and Belgium, the evacuation would have resulted in much higher losses in ships and men than was actually the case.

The Hurricanes and Spitfires over the Channel were also helped by Hudsons. On 28 May No 220 Squadron proceeded by air on attachment to join No 206 Squadron at Bircham Newton for operational duties. All available pilots moved with the squadron. While at Bircham Newton the squadron maintained two standing patrols during daylight hours; one, carried out by single aircraft, was between Ijmuiden and Texel to look out for enemy warships and E-boats preceding them down the Channel towards Dunkirk; the other patrol was between North Foreland, Calais and Dunkirk to protect troops on the beach and the ships of all types evacuating the troops across the Channel from Dunkirk from aerial attack by German dive-bombers and low-flying aircraft.

Jim Pedersen was one of the 220 Squadron pilots and while over Dover his aircraft was fired on by 'friendly' anti-aircraft guns! He followed this up by chasing two Heinkel 111's to the Belgian coast. His log book entry read: '. . . Heavy flak and machine gun fire from the German and British held beaches – did not close range sufficiently to engage the He 111 – fired on by two Hurricanes. . .' The Hudson pilots reported that the Channel was absolutely thick with craft of all kinds, destroyers, trawlers, tugs and barges, minesweepers, pleasure-cruisers, weekend motor launches and rowing boats going to and fro taking Allied troops to England.

The Hudsons from Bircham Newton were over the beaches on three long patrols during the day although the visibility was bad. There were occasional heavy rain showers and this was probably the reason that few enemy aircraft were seen, although there was anti-aircraft fire from the Belgian coast. A Hudson from No 206 Squadron

A Hudson protecting the 'little ships' from aerial attack off Dunkirk. This photograph shows vividly the vast activity that saved the troops to fight another day.

spotted a U-boat off the Dutch coast heading towards Dunkirk and attacked it.

Again on the next day there were three battle patrols of three Hudsons over the Channel and enemy bombers were chased away from the vicinity of the troop transports, but Hudson Z-Zebra was itself chased by two enemy aircraft. Hudsons from No 220 Squadron reported heavy German bombing at Dunkirk in the afternoon, which included an attack on a hospital ship.

Hudsons from Nos 206 and 220 Squadrons were again over the Channel the following day and despite heavy anti-aircraft fire from both Dunkirk and Ostend, no hits were made on the aircraft. A He111 was attacked and several bursts were seen to enter the aircraft which dived to escape, jettisoning its bombs at the same time.

Jim Pedersen was again active on the last two days of the month, he recorded:

> May 30 and another Dover patrol . . . attacked an He111, starboard engine damaged, having to return on one motor – anti-aircraft fire on the beaches – rear gunners of the He111 very good shots – Hudsons not sufficiently fast to conduct proper attack – two other Hudsons also hit – when jettisoning bombs, these exploded while flying at 100 feet, resultant gain of height was startling. . . .

Then the following entry:

> 31 May . . . Dover patrol – photo recce of beaches at Dunkirk – attacked by a Hurricane two separate times. . . .

On 1 June a flight of three Hudsons from 220 Squadron intercepted a force of 40 enemy aircraft, mostly Ju87 Stukas, attacking shipping in the Channel. Hudson K-King made two attacks and shot down two dive bombers with the front guns. South Africans Ronald Selley and Aubrey Haarhoff, pilot and gunner respectively, flew the Hudson. While the Spitfires patrolling above the cloud at 4,000 feet failed to see the German aircraft the three Hudsons were ordered to break formation and attack. Pilot Officer Selley sped off to engage eight Ju87's that were about five miles away. Flying Officer Haarhoff said afterwards:

As we approached we could see them circling in about a two mile radius, each doing a steep climb with a stall turn at the top and then came over in a very steep dive straight down with such regularity that it might have been a Hendon flying display.

Selley said :

I will never forget it as long as I live. We saw about forty altogether and they seemed to split up into bunches of about twenty. I took a bunch of eight which had twelve more flying at 200 feet above them.

Regardless of the great risk the pilot flew alone in that ring of twenty enemies. It might have been a flying circus with a South African ringmaster. Round and round he went with them. He attempted to dive with one but soon found that it was too steep for the Hudson, he then waited for his attack to coincide with the moment that the aircraft climbed before doing its stall-turn and dive.

We attacked as one came up and as he stall turned we just leaped across and shot him down [said the pilot]. As we circled them we picked them off going round and as they came up I got them with the front guns. I shot down two with my front guns and damaged another, but we did not see that one go in.

The extraordinary thing was that the Hudson was not hit. There was a mention in a contemporary aeronautical magazine that during the engagement with the Stukas some of them attempted to bomb the Hudsons. Pilot Officer Selley and Flying Officer Haarhoff were both awarded the DFC for this action, the other members of the crew were Sergeant Fletcher and Leading Aircraftman Richardson. Ronald Selley said he would not forget the incident 'as long as I live'; tragically this was not very long, for a few months later after transferring to No 233 Squadron he died in a flying accident.

It will be remembered that three Hudsons were engaged in the attack. Hudson G-George attacked three Stukas that dived past, the pilot giving the rear gunner the opportunity to fire at them, one was claimed shot down and the other two damaged. Just as the third Hudson was about to engage another Stuka, a flight of Spitfires arrived and for one moment it appeared that they were about to

shoot down the Hudsons. A recognition signal had to be fired and
in the process the Spitfires' plan of attack was upset and no enemy
aircraft was shot down.

Jim Pedersen was also active on this day, but in a bombing role :

> Crossover patrol off Texel – starboard engine damaged by anti-
> aircraft fire – returned early – starboard constant speed unit hit
> by shell splinters – flack very good – three salvos fired before the
> first shells burst. . . .

These indeed were hectic days for all the armed forces as the Battle
for France turned into the Battle of Britain. On 2 June seven
Hudsons proceeded to Detling to stand by in case they should be
needed as a fighter patrol. They were debombed and ready for action
but were not called upon during the day to take any action. They
returned to Bircham Newton in the evening carrying out a patrol
along the Dutch coast, the object of which was to locate E-boats.
Although the Hudson was a useful long distance reconnaissance
aircraft which could carry a good quantity of bombs for offensive
purposes and was armed with twin guns in the front turret and a
sting in the tail, to think of its being pressed into service as a fighter
leaves one in awe.

On 3 June a force of seven Hudsons from 220 Squadron carried
out a night bombing raid on oil tanks at Rotterdam from between
8,000 and 12,000 feet. Large fires were seen burning in the area but
anti-aircraft fire was heavy and intense and many of the aircraft,
which all returned safely, were damaged by shrapnel. Jim Pedersen
entered in his log book 'Rotterdam bombing raid – came out through
Belgium – extreme difficulty in locating target – held by a great
number of searchlights – flak above the Hague very intense'. The
squadron scribe recorded :

> Seven aircraft of this squadron carried out a night raid on oil
> tanks at Rotterdam. The seven aircraft took off at the same time
> and split into two flights. After reaching the Dutch coast at two
> different places the aircraft split up and made individual attacks
> on the target from different directions and different heights and
> at varying time intervals. It is thought that the result of the
> attack was successful as the target area was definitely located and
> large fires were seen to be left burning in this area.

A Hudson on patrol over Dunkirk in June 1940. An immense column of black smoke rises from the oil depot after two of the tanks had been fired. In the foreground can be seen the wide beach and shallow sea from which thousands of men of the BEF had to embark.

By 4 June the evacuation was completed; on the previous four days Coastal Command made 327 sorties over or near the Dunkirk coast. One must realise that this severe fighting was being conducted by general reconnaissance pilots and crews with no specialised fighter training, flying aircraft neither designed for the purpose nor possessed of the greater speed of their adversaries.

Of Dunkirk, Jim was reported as saying :

The sight from the air beggars description, the deafening din, continuous explosions, accompanied by burning houses, burning ships, bursting shells and bombs, and fires everywhere, a pall of smoke by day and a vivid inferno by night. The German planes attacked in large numbers, flight after flight, and although greatly outnumbered, our planes proved better fighters all along the line.

The squadron entry for 4 June says:

> The evacuation of Dunkirk having been completed, the squadron did not carry out any operational trips but remained at Bircham Newton. Three aircraft and their crews returned to Thornaby.

The entry for the following day was: 'The remainder of the squadron who were at Bircham Newton returned to Thornaby and all personnel who had been at Bircham Newton, both flying and ground staff were granted 48 hours leave from the end of the day.' Never was leave harder earned. The troops may well have asked 'Where was the Royal Air Force?' at Dunkirk, but the sturdy Hudsons were over the Channel throughout, acting as both bomber and fighter and as a deterrent to the Luftwaffe.

V

Atlantic Air Bridge

In the early days of the war the Hudsons ordered from America were taking three months from the time they were test-flown until they reached their operational destination in Britain. In the middle of 1940 it was thought that they could possibly be flown across the Atlantic thereby saving valuable shipping space and avoiding losses at sea. Already in 1939 the postal authorities of Britain, Canada and the USA had looked at the possibilities of starting a regular air service across the Atlantic, but it was thought that it would have to close down during the winter months. The need to have the Hudsons quickly meant that the possibility of winter crossings had to be investigated, and to this end a party of British Overseas Airway Corporation captains were sent across the Atlantic. Among the party was Captain D. C. T. Bennett, an Australian who had left his native land in 1930, travelled to Britain and joined the RAF. He left the Service in 1935 as a qualified pilot, navigator, ground engineer, wireless operator and instructor. Now, in 1940, all these qualifications would be needed for this new venture.

The springboard for the Atlantic flight was a new airfield recently constructed in Newfoundland called Gander, after a nearby lake. Conditions were primitive and the British pilots were accommodated in railway sleeping cars adjacent to the hangars.

On arrival Captain Bennett and a colleague went to the Lockheed plant in Burbank, California, where they were told that the first long-range Hudson would be ready by the middle of September, followed shortly afterwards by another fifty. Captain Bennett test-flew the Hudson and persuaded the Lockheed authorities to fit an extra fuel tank in the fuselage. Both captains then flew back to Canada in the first two Hudsons for air delivery. Because of the United States neutrality regulations – this was 1940 – they travelled as passengers behind American pilots. Again due to these neutrality regulations the Hudsons landed at American airfields and were dragged over the border between America and Canada by horses.

47

(Horses will, incidentally, figure in the Hudson story again later in the book.)

With the aircraft promised from Lockheed it was time to find pilots and wireless operators to conduct the Hudsons across the Atlantic. The former were quite easy to find but there was some difficulty finding radio men. It was here that Captain Bennett's wide qualifications were invaluable. He was able to test the applicants and ensure that only those suitable were hired. For the pilots the two Hudsons that had already arrived were used as trainers. Captain Bennett records:

> Day after day dual instruction was carried out on the Hudsons which had some very tricky characteristics, including an ability to drop a wing if bounced and quite a nasty stall if one was so stupid as to get too slow. It is not being unduly rude to say that the Hudson was a fine performer, but a handful, which could be extremely dangerous if one were careless.

Finally seven Hudsons were ready for the big day. Captain Bennett was to lead, and his pre-flight preparations had been prodigious. A flight plan had been made out for each aircraft, he had made up cruising cards for the hours spent on consumption tests and the weather maps and forecasts had been carefully studied. This flight, due to leave on 10 November, would be the first time that any air crossing had been attempted over the Atlantic so late in the year.

There was a band to see them off, the chorus of aircraft engines drowned the music as the Hudsons took off into the dark beyond. Captain Bennett circled the airfield while the Hudsons formed up on him. The navigation of the flight to England depended on him. An extract from a diary kept by one of the radio officers of this historic flight reads:

> For the first hour there seemed to be planes all around us, we found oil leaking badly from the starboard tank and I passed a message to the leader, Captain Bennett, that our oil tank had ruptured but we were watching closely and would keep him advised. Finally we found the oil flow was diminishing and decided to go on but found ourselves quite alone. When the skipper chose to go on we climbed up to 16,000 feet, which afterwards proved a

smart move as we gained on the rest right from there. What with the excitement of the take-off and leaking oil tank, I was glad to sit back and relax and I think I actually enjoyed myself. Just after 0200 our bomb bay tank ran dry and both motors started cutting out. We were not expecting it and both the pilot and co-pilot went for the hand pump and gas valve. I don't think anything ever sounded so good to me as hearing those big Wrights hit their stride again and settle down to a steady drone. From then on the Skipper didn't need to watch any gauges.

At 0225 we were at 18,000 feet, and we must have looked funny sitting there with a rubber tube stuck in our mouths. I sometimes get scared when I think of how we started out that first trip with one little tank of oxygen and nothing but a rubber tube to suck it through. The pilot did the regulating and knew what he was doing, as none of us suffered any ill effects, although at one time I felt my stomach would cave in and the pilot got down in the nose and had trouble getting up. I didn't know until afterwards why he turned the oxygen full-on for a few seconds.

The Skipper had been losing altitude, and when at 0500 he couldn't get contact at 2,000 feet, he pulled back up to 6,000 feet and stayed there. We were in rain cloud off and on: after the cold of 18,000 feet, we were forced to take off our heavy clothing as it was quite warm. Even cutting off the heat didn't seem to cool the Hudson off, and for a time I was in my shirt sleeves.

Wireless silence was kept east of 20 degrees west but when it was broken the operators were unable to read through the static. This aircraft was the third to arrive at Aldergrove airport, near Belfast, and landed at 0850. The flight as a whole was successful and all seven Hudsons arrived safely although one come in late after first landing at another airfield. The next day the Hudsons were flown across to Squire's Gate at Blackpool to be serviced by the base there. The aircraft crews, with the exception of their leader who went later, were transhipped back to Canada the next day.

The second Atlantic flight of Hudsons left on 29 November. There was a temperature of 16 degrees Fahrenheit at the airport and it was with difficulty that the engines of the Hudsons were brought to life. The aircraft had to be literally dug out of deep snow, before being cleared of ice to enable them to take off. Again all seven

This Hudson III 'Spirit of Lockheed Vega employees' was flown to England by Captain Donald Bennett. Varley Allan Pedersen (*inset*) also flew aircraft across the Atlantic, he features as 'The Kiwi'.

arrived safely. The third flight left in the middle of December and once more all arrived safely the next day – the 'Atlantic Air Bridge' was now firmly established.

The workers from the Lockheed plant in California presented a Hudson to the people of Britain as a Christmas gift. This aircraft christened 'Spirit of Lockheed Vega' was flown by Captain Bennett leading the fourth and what was to be the last of group flights of Hudsons to Britain and arrived on 29 December – just seven days after leaving the factory! This flight was the first that was not successful as only four Hudsons arrived, one had crashed on take-off blocking another and a third returned to Gander with engine trouble.

Jim Pedersen, the New Zealander we have already met joined the Trans-Atlantic Ferry pool early in 1941 and on 21 January flew in a Hudson with Captain Bennett on an air test at 24,000 feet without oxygen over St Hubert airport at Montreal; the effects of the lack of oxygen made him feel slightly drunk. Jim was among the earliest batch of RAF crews to be sent to the pool, the first left England in December 1940. Flight Lieutenant Ian Patterson was another early arrival at the pool, he had just completed a long tour with No 269 Squadron and had already flown a total of 157 sorties, he recalls:

'My posting from No 269 Squadron had been the result of a signal from the Air Ministry asking for a crew to be sent to America where they would be trained on B17 Boeing aircraft and then fly one that had been bought by Britain, back to this country.

'I stepped out of my Hudson at Dyce aerodrome after flying from Wick and heaped my baggage beside me on the tarmac. I managed to spend that evening in Aberdeen at the Caledonian Hotel and then caught the night train for London the following afternoon. I took the tube from Piccadilly and reported to Uxbridge for embarkation orders.

'The arrangements at this RAF depot were the same as they have always been, in a hell of a mess, nobody knew anything about us. At this time I was worried, but the following four months were to be such a succession of journeys from pillar to post under bungling leadership, I soon learned not to worry. Two days later I met up with chaps who had been posted from other squadrons to go to America, mostly they came from Coastal Command but there were a couple from the Photographic Reconnaissance Unit. Suddenly news came through that we were to catch the 2115 train that night from Euston to Glasgow and there was a terrific scramble to get there in time.

'When we arrived in Glasgow the following morning we were sent by another train to Gourock, where with a lot more servicemen we went aboard a small boat and were ferried downstream to the *Leopoldville*, the troopship that was to carry us to Canada.

'Conditions aboard the ship were very poor, for example I shared a small cabin with four other chaps. However, the food turned out to be excellent. Most of the passengers consisted of a School of General Reconnaissance which was being transferred to Canada.

'We cast off on Wednesday afternoon 18 December and began our journey down the Clyde to join the convoy. The next morning the coastline was receding into the distance. There were a lot of orders and restrictions to be obeyed on the ship and there was the usual discomfort of travelling at sea in wartime, such as lifebelts worn at all times, nobody being allowed on deck after blackout, cameras collected and no diaries allowed. With our fast speed we left the convoy well behind and HMS *Royal Sovereign* escorted us from mid-Atlantic to Halifax, Nova Scotia.

'The sea became rougher and rougher with Christmas Eve being the worst night and Christmas the worst day. Early on Saturday a Hudson from Canada arrived and escorted us until he was relieved by two Stranraer flying boats, so we knew we could not be far from land, and by early afternoon it was in sight. Two hours later *Leopoldville* entered Halifax harbour. Needless to say, we spent that night in town.

'Our stay in Halifax turned into weeks before any further news of our forthcoming visit to the States was announced and in the meantime our party managed to 'do' Montreal pretty thoroughly, finding that the eight dollars a day subsistence we were receiving had to be watched carefully to make it last. Finally we boarded a train for Los Angeles where we were met by a Wing Commander who had a bus waiting which took us the seventy miles to Riverside where we alighted at our destination, a hotel called the Mission Inn. Each day we were collected and taken the eight miles to March Field a United States Army Air Corps aerodrome where there were three squadrons, the 23rd, 30th and 90th bombardment squadrons; all were equipped with Boeing aircraft of a type, earlier, though similar, to those which we were to take to England. It was exceedingly pleasant at March Field, the sun shone every day and we enjoyed all the pleasures we had been deprived of during the long months of war in Britain.

'On the second day of my stay I was taken for a flight down to Tucson, Arizona, near the Mexican border. A couple of days later I went on a flight when bombs were dropped on a sea marker just off Catalina Island, and during the week flew to 21,000 feet over the Muroc Range to drop more bombs from that height. Now and then I managed to snatch a little dual. I was then teamed up with an Irishman and we were checked out as first pilots, day, and were sent to Sacramento where we took night landings. While at McCelland Field in Sacramento we flew over to San Francisco and admired the Golden Gate bridge. Later we journeyed up to Seattle in Washington to take delivery of the aircraft we were to ferry to England.

'On 18 March 1941 we took delivery of a Boeing B17C and started off. We were in company with two other machines and each of us had a US Army Air Corps officer on board to overcome the formalities caused by British aviators flying in neutral America. Our trip was to be made in easy stages, and owing to insurance, was not to be undertaken at night or in bad weather. That night we stopped at Portland, Oregon, and there we experienced our first taste of what the press was going to be like on our way home – we were hounded. The following day we flew to Boise, Idaho, on the second stage of our trip and owing to deteriorating weather conditions were kept there for two days before we continued on to Salt Lake City, Utah. Bad weather again lengthened our stay as we waited for decent conditions to cross the Rocky mountains but then we were off on the fourth stage of our trip and landed at Kansas City, Missouri, and next day we flew on to Dayton, Ohio.

'Our stay at Wright Field was lengthy as we had another inspection of the machine, had it camouflaged and the compass swung when more spares had been taken aboard. We flew it locally and re-swung the compass in the air and checked the directional gyro which had become unserviceable on the way across the States, and a test for leakage in the manifold, then took the machine up to 31,000 feet. All this in preparation for the journey across the Atlantic. We finally left Wright Field and made the interesting flight up the lakes and over Niagara Falls to Montreal. Two days later we were sent off to Newfoundland, by this time we were convinced that the capabilities and comfort of the aircraft at heights and over long distances were remarkably good.

'On Good Friday, 11 April 1941 the morning dawned fine. Upon inspection, in the light of day, of the building in which we had spent the night, we saw a sign over the front door which read 'Eastbound Inn', obviously the accommodation had been built there by the Canadian Pacific railway people for the express purpose of housing ferry pilots while they waited for favourable conditions to fly to England.

'Between the building, which faced the field and the runways, was a hangar and immediately on the right of this was a rather older building which was used as an administration block, and it was to this place that we wound our way to receive a preliminary forecast of the Atlantic conditions. The outlook for that evening was splendid and accordingly preparations were made for the flight; these consisted of roughly a flight plan and aircraft check, provision of rations and dozens of other small details. In the early evening we ate an early supper of bacon and eggs and then saying goodbye, climbed aboard and taxied out. Just then the second Fortress landed from Montreal.

'Disappointment was to overtake us, for, as we were about to turn down the runway there was a loud bang, the aircraft lurched, and we realised that the starboard tyre had blown out. Of course, we were not going to accept defeat that easily, and we tried desperately to fit a new wheel, but darkness caught us and we abandoned the flight for twenty-four hours. We went through the same procedures again and although the weather forecast for the trip was good there was some low cloud over the British Isles and accordingly we signalled to England in the morning, a request for Regional Control frequencies with the aid of which we hoped to cross Britain and let down somewhere over the North Sea. We had the range to accomplish this comfortably and knowing the east coast so well, we anticipated no difficulty in approaching from that side. Our estimation of the flying time to Ireland was about nine and a half hours and perhaps another hour and a half to the North Sea.

'The flight was postponed for a further day when the weather conditions were not satisfactory and by this time the Canadian Pacific Railway cook was getting annoyed at cutting sandwiches for us every afternoon.

'On Sunday 13 April 1941 it was again fine at Gander airport although very cold. The preliminary weather report of conditions over the Atlantic sounded well so once more we made arrangements for the flight.

'It was decided that we should fly on a Great Circle track to Ireland and a chart was made out accordingly for each of the ten zones into which the Atlantic was divided, and a copy of this was submitted to the controller at Newfoundland. Weather reports came in the form of ten sheets, each one containing information on cloud, temperatures, icing conditions, winds, etc, and divided in such a way that we could readily pick a favourable route.

'Our machine had been run out of the hangar, we ate our bacon and eggs and boarded. After testing the engines we moved to the long runway and took about a mile, using 1200 horse power from each of the four engines and with the air speed indicator showing 135 mph we lifted the wheels from the ground and the Fortress's twenty-two and a half tons became airborne very easily and started climbing immediately to 15,000 feet while turning on course. At 0626 the following morning the Fortress landed at Ayr in a record time of 8 hours 42 minutes. About half-an-hour later the second Fortress landed. At that time of the morning the airfield was almost deserted and the few workmen present did not grasp that they had witnessed an historic event, that of the first Flying Fortress ever to land in the British Isles.

'We were later ordered to fly the aircraft to Squire's Gate, Blackpool, and the arrival of a Flying Fortress at that station seemed to call forth a lot of attention, and also an officer in charge of duty transport who came bounding across the field and made a pantomime that we were to follow him to a parking place, which turned out to be Vickers Armstrong's hangar. Here we removed our bags and were taken along to the St Anne's Hotel for the night.

'We later caught a train to London and gave details of our flight to Air Ministry officials.'

Here we leave Ian Patterson for the moment and catch up with Jim Pedersen. While in the States, Jim, like many other visitors, went around the film studios. He toured the MGM studio where he was photographed with Greer Garson, Walter Pidgeon and Ann Southern. Greer Garson asked Jim to post a bundle of letters for her in England. Returning to the job in hand Jim's Fortress was accepted under Lease-Lend at the end of March 1941, then there was more flying between Boeing and McCord Fields. Jim covered much the same ground as

Hudson 1 of No 11 Bomber Reconnaissance Squadron RCAF over the Gulf of St Lawrence in 1940.

Hudson 1 aircraft of No 13 Squadron RCAF off the coast of British Columbia in 1941.

Ian Patterson before him until leaving for the British Isles on 15 May, the log book entry reads:

Gander – England transatlantic crossing at 21,000 feet – Good weather – ice formed on the inside of the navigators compartment – picked up German radio programme one hour out of Newfoundland.

The time of the flight from Canada to Scotland was nine hours forty-five minutes, of which four hours was night flying. Jim flew back to Montreal later in the month and after air testing several Hudsons eventually flew up to Gander before flying Hudson AM800 across the Atlantic. Flying Officer Bill Tacon was among other ferry people in Montreal at this time. The Hudson Jim flew to Scotland ended up in North Africa and was struck off charge at the end of October 1943. Jim's brief log entry for the flight was: 'Newfoundland to England – transatlantic crossing at 11,000 feet – iceburgs sighted.' The trip was of 11 hours 20 minutes duration, of which four was made at night. Later Jim returned to Montreal to pilot Hudson AM845 to Britain; this aircraft was destroyed in action while in service with No 500 Squadron on 9 February 1942. This flight on 16 July was made in company with twenty other aircraft. In this month of July 1941 the Atlantic Air Bridge came under the command of the newly formed Royal Air Force Ferry Command, and later in the year the airfield at Dorval became the home of the new organisation. Captain Bennett had by this time left the Atlantic Ferry to take over other work and it came as a shock to him when he later learned that as many as six Hudsons had been lost on trips between Canada and Britain, largely as a result of inadequate preparations to avoid icing.

By mid-1941 airmen were being trained in Canada under the Commonwealth Joint Air Training Plan, and the Empire Air Training scheme covered the basic training of pilots, air gunners, wireless operators, navigators and observers. Over eighty airfields were used in Canada alone and men from Britain, Australia, New Zealand and the Dominions were turned out as fully trained aircrew. After initial training, and later in 'grading', future pilots moved on to service flying schools after a few weeks at the elementary flying schools. The Australians went straight to the service flying schools as they received their elementary and initial training in their own country. The training included flying both night and day, solo and dual, map-reading, instrument-flying, bombing and gunnery.

The high level of training achieved is exemplified by the fact that the majority of Hudson crews ferried their own aircraft back across the Atlantic after completing 250 hours training. Back in the United Kingdom the crews continued training on operational type aircraft at OTU's up and down the country.

Some of the future Coastal Command crews remained in Canada for general reconnaissance training at one of the schools established there. There were two schools on Prince Edward Island in the Gulf of St Lawrence, one at Debest, New Brunswick, and another at Greenwood, Nova Scotia.

The Captain Bennett mentioned in the chapter is, of course, better known as the commander of the Path Finder Force, which he led after re-joining the RAF; he finally retired as Air Vice Marshal D. C. T. Bennett CB CBE DSO.

Bill Tacon, too, had a remarkable career later in the war and after it – including some later work with Hudsons. He was posted to his native New Zealand early in 1943. On 1 March he took over as commander of No 1 General Reconnaissance Squadron at Whenuapi, Auckland and on 10 May took over a similar appointment with No 4 Squadron at Nausori, Fiji. Despite his elevated position Bill continued to fly Hudsons. In June and July his squadron was employed in submarine searching and escort duties. In September Bill escorted the Governor General from Norfolk Island. Japanese submarines were still very active in the autumn and Hudsons were despatched searching for them, or escorting ships unfortunate enough to have been torpedoed.

At the beginning of December Bill flew the Governor of Fiji from Tuausori to Ellice Island and the next day flew on to Tarani on Gilbert Island arriving just eight days after the island had been recaptured from the Japanese.

To round off the story of Bill Tacon we follow him back to England where he converted to Beaufighters, again in a mast-height attacking role, until he was shot down in the autumn of 1944 and spent an uncomfortable few months as a prisoner-of-war in the hell hole of Stalag Luft in Barth Pomerania, until the liberation.

Bill Tacon flew Hudson EK769 in Dorval, Canada as late as the end of 1945; six years of flying Hudsons, over 1,800 hours on this type of aircraft alone!

Hudson of No 11 Squadron RCAF showing an adapted turret position for navigational training. The other aircraft is a Douglas Digby.

The only safe way for a Hudson to be on water – aboard a scow. A Hudson 1 in Canada.

In 1947, as a member of the King's Flight, Bill Tacon flew His Majesty King George VI, Princess Elizabeth, Princess Margaret and the Duke of Edinburgh in South Africa. This Hudson pilot extraordinaire retired from the Royal Air Force in 1971 as Air Commodore E. W. Tacon CBE DSO MVO DFC and bar AFC.

VI

Fat, Friendly Hudson

At the beginning of World War II the 17,000 ton P and O liner *Rawalpindi* was one of several liners taken over by the Admiralty and converted to an armed merchant cruiser by the addition of 6-in guns. Captain E. C. Kennedy was brought back from retirement and given command of the ship. On 23 November 1939 while *Rawalpindi* was patrolling the Iceland-Faeroes strait the German battle-cruiser *Scharnhorst* was sighted at dusk; a one-sided action lasting 14 minutes took place at 8,000 yards before the AMC was sunk. The gallant captain was lost with his ship, but not before his gunners had succeeded in hitting the battle-cruiser.

Captain Kennedy's son, Ludovic, was serving in the Royal Navy at the time and eighteen months later, as a sub-lieutenant, was himself involved in the sinking of the powerful German battleship *Bismarck*. Ludovic Kennedy was serving aboard the Tribal Class destroyer *Tartar* and was to be grateful to the Lockheed Hudson before his ship docked. Sub-Lieutenant Kennedy, later to become better known as an author, broadcaster and television personality, wrote of the event 'as a hobby to pass away many dreary hours at sea'.

I think that all of us were willing to acknowledge the gallantry of the enemy. For the past five days the crew of *Bismarck* had been almost continually at action stations. She had been shadowed by our cruisers for nearly two days, shadowed and attacked by aircraft and, the night before the battle, subjected to a torpedo attack by the Fourth Flotilla. All through that night her crew must have known that dawn would bring the British battle fleet and, for most of them, death. I do not think you will find one British sailor present at the battle who will not admit that *Bismarck* fought a very gallant fight.

We left just before the end of the action. I took a last look at

Bismarck as we steamed away. Through my glasses I could see great, jagged holes in her sides and superstructure, through which tongues of flame were shooting; she was listing heavily to port, emitting a column of black smoke. Her guns were awry, some of them pointing meaninglessly to the sky. It was a terrible sight. *Bismarck* had been a majestic and powerful ship; she was a charred and battered wreck.

All of us were relieved that the tension of the last four days was lifted, and showed our relief by pointless, good-humoured banter in the wardroom. For me, perhaps the battle had a more personal meaning than for the others; I felt I had been something more than a privileged spectator at a great sea fight. My mind went back to a cold, dark evening in November 1939, when an armed merchant-cruiser had gone down in flames at the hands of another German battleship, her guns firing and her colours flying to the last.

And I felt, somehow, that I had seen *Rawalpindi* avenged. . . .

Ludovic Kennedy slept well, the next thing he heard was the messenger calling him : 'Half-past seven, sir ! Wake up, Mr Kennedy, sir, it's half-past seven and you've got the forenoon watch !'

'I turn over in my bunk sleepily'. 'All right, messenger, I'm awake. Is the navigating officer keeping relieve decks?'

' "Yes sir. You will be required on the bridge at half-past eight." '

'I lie in my bunk for a few minutes, my mind full of the events of the last four days. What a chase *Bismarck* led us, and what a sight the battle was ! We shall be in harbour by this evening and, if I know the Captain, there will be some party.

'I hoist myself out of my bunk and go to the washstand to get the sleep out of my eyes and brush my teeth. I pull on my trousers, get into my reefer and brush my hair. Then I hurry to the wardroom for breakfast.

'Broad, the duty steward, is sitting in one of the armchairs reading *Life*. "Come on, Broad," I say, "I want my breakfast. Is it ready?"

' "Just coming down, sir" says Broad; this is his stock answer to enquiries about food. What he really means is, "It will be placed in front of you as soon as I go up to the galley and collect it from that fat cook."

'I drink a cup of tea while Broad is up at the galley and switch on the wireless. A man is encouraging me to grip the bars of a chair and kick my legs sideways in time with the music he is going to play. In a few minutes Broad comes down with breakfast.

'I am well into my second egg when Guns, who has been having the morning watch, comes in for a cup of tea before changing. "What's it like up there this morning?" I ask him.

' "Grand!" says Guns. "Sun's shining, not too cold, quite dry on the bridge. Captain's in a good temper and all's well with the world. We ought to be in by tea-time."

' "What price the Locarno this evening?" I ask him.

' "No, just a few pints in a quiet little pub will do me nicely, I think," says Guns.

' "And with a nice quiet little something to hold your hand, I daresay."

' "I'm a respectable married man, I am," says Guns, winking. "Yes, indeed!" He winks again.

'I finish my breakfast and go back to my cabin for my duffel-coat, gloves and binoculars, I come out on to the quarterdeck and make my way forward.

'It is a crisp, bright morning, much the same as yesterday though there are more clouds in the sky, and the wind is stronger. It biffs me hard from the other side of the funnel-casing and machine-gun bridge as I walk along the upper deck.

' "Morning Spider," I say, as I climb on to the compass platform beside him. "What's happening?"

' "Nothing much," Spider answers. "Course 206, speed 15 knots, 142 revolutions. HA cruising stations. *Mashona* a mile on the starboard beam."

'*Mashona* is our chummy ship, and no doubt we will celebrate with her when we get in this evening.

'I am just going to take over the watch officially from Spider when I see him looking intently through his glasses towards the starboard quarter. "I don't like the look of that," he says. "Can you see what it is?"

'I raise my glasses and train them in the same direction. Almost immediately, a big, black, four-engined aeroplane appears in the field of vision. I can see the black crosses on the fuselage distinctly.

' "Christ, yes," I say "It's a mucking Wulf!"

' "I'll tell the Master," Spider says. "You ring the alarm bells."

'I go to the front of the bridge and press the alarm push: *short long, short long, short long* – the signal for anti-aircraft action stations.

'When the Captain reaches the bridge I run down to my action station at the pom-pom. My crew are manning the telephones, seeing that the feed belts are in order, setting the levers to fire. I climb to the middle of the platform between the trainer and captain of the gun and the layer.

'The Focke-Wulf cruises round, but remains at some distance, out of range of the main armament. I post look-outs on either quarter in case dive-bombers come shooting out of the low clouds. Keeping a watchful eye all round I await further developments. 'I do not have to wait long; the port look-out reports an aircraft approaching from the port beam. I look up, and recognise it as a Heinkel 111. A moment later, Number One in the Director lets fly with the main armament. That scares the pilot, for he turns away without finishing his run.

' "Aircraft to starboard, sir," shouts one of the loading numbers.

' "Train right," I order.

'The trainer moves his handle as fast as he can, and in a few seconds the gun is brought round to face the starboard bow. Two Heinkel 111's are approaching, about three thousand feet up on a level course. The main armament is training round to engage, but they will not be able to get off a salvo in time. It is up to us.

'I wait until the planes are within effective gun range, then give the order, "Open fire!" The staccato bark of the guns usually deafens me; now I can hardly hear it. I am too intent on watching those black vultures coming to the end of their run.

'Now I can see the bombs falling. They are specks at first, like sparrows' eggs, but grow larger every second. The Captain has seen them, too, for we are moving faster and heeling over to port as we swing to starboard. I clutch the stanchion and watch the bombs, fascinated.

' "It's all right, chaps," I yell, "they won't hit us!"

'*Woomph, woomph, woomph*; the bombs have landed in our wake and have burst with tremendous detonations. The Captain brings the ship back to her original course, and by the low-pitched whine from the gearing-room I can tell that we are reducing speed.

'We have hardly finished engaging this pair when two more appear on the port bow. And so it goes on; the guns fire, the aircraft drop their bombs, the ship swings to port or starboard, and the bombs land in the sea, sometimes quite far away, at other times too close to be comfortable.

'During a lull a petty officer turns and says: "Looks as though they've hit *Mashona*, sir!" Poor old *Mashona*! She has taken a list to port, and clouds of steam are rising from abreast the break of the fo'c'sle. The list increases, and she has soon stopped altogether. Thank God, those filthy aeroplanes are giving us a respite now just when we need it!

'We close to within two cables of *Mashona*, which has now listed over forty degrees, and I intercept a signal from her, "Abandoning ship". A little later, figures can be seen sliding down her hull into the water.

'I go down to the upper deck to help Number One superintend the placing of nets over the ship's side. The cooks have left their supply parties and are preparing hot soup in the galleys. The doctor is turning the wardroom into a second sick-bay. Blankets are being stripped from the officers' bunks and piled in a corner.

'The first survivors reach the ship. We haul them up the netting and deposit them on the upper deck, where their wet clothes are stripped from their shivering bodies. They are wrapped in blankets and taken to the wardroom or the Captain's day-cabin to be rubbed down. Some of the older men have not the strength to cover the whole journey; when they have almost reached the netting they seem to think that they are saved and do not bother to exert themselves more. This is fatal, because they begin to sink at once and then they must make an even greater effort to right themselves.

'For a whole hour we lie stopped, while exhausted men, in twos and threes, reach the ship's side and are helped on board. Last off his ship is *Mashona's* captain; he is pushing two exhausted men on a rubber cushion in front of him, and from time to time stops to wave his ship's battle-ensign and shout encouragement to the others.

'We are all wondering what has happened to the German bombers. Surely they must return soon; and God help us when they do!

'*Mashona* is lying on her side now, motionless and broken, like a wounded animal awaiting the end. We steam slowly away, leaving another destroyer, which has just joined us, to send her to the bottom by gunfire. We set course for harbour.

'I go down to the wardroom to give the doctor a hand, but have not been there more than a few minutes when I hear the cry:

'Aircraft approaching from astern!' I am up at the pom-pom in a flash, and see another He111 flying dead up the stern. As soon as it reaches its position of bomb-release the Captain begins to swing the ship. The bombs start falling – *one, two, three, four, five,* I count. They seem to be coming straight at us. Christ! They *are* going to hit us!

'I hear myself shouting automatically, as I have done before: "It's all right! They've missed again!" Then the bombs land; they fall in a little clump not fifty feet off the port quarter. They make no noise and there are no explosions – just five little *phuts* as they disappear beneath the surface.

'We are attacked all that afternoon, not incessantly but at about ten-minute intervals. I don't feel frightened while we are being attacked; I am too fascinated by what is happening, too busy giving orders to my crew. Fear comes during the lulls; it is when I hear the cry "Aircraft approaching" that I feel weak inside. It is the same feeling I had at school, waiting outside the headmaster's study to be beaten – a sickly, sinking sensation in the stomach. Only it is not as bad as then, because at school I wasn't allowed to alter course and increase speed to avoid what was coming to me; I knew I had to take it.

'Everyone is asking where our fighters are. We have been in sight of the Irish coast for two or three hours, and there is still no sign of them. During a lull at about five o'clock, a petty officer comes round with hot tea and ship's biscuits, the first food of the day for most of us. We crunch the dry biscuits hungrily and swallow gulps of the hot, sweet tea. After a cigarette we feel like new men.

'Soon after, while a new attack is developing, we see a Hudson streaking across the sky – the first friendly aircraft that has been near us. It goes straight for an He111 which is about to attack the other destroyer, now four miles astern of us. Streams of smoke pour out of the Heinkel's fuselage, and we watch it plunge into the sea. A roar goes up from every man in the ship.

'Just before nightfall another Hudson arrives to escort us into harbour. It circles around until dark, chasing off two more Heinkels which are manoeuvring to attack. There is something unbelievably comforting in that fat, friendly, protecting form. I feel I would like to fall on the pilot's neck and weep with gratitude.

'We enter harbour at midnight and make fast alongside the oiler. I walk stiffly down to the wardroom, which looks like the remains of a jumble-sale. "A whisky and soda, Broad," I say, "and make it a double."

' "Aye, aye, sir," says Broad. "No party tonight, I'm afraid, sir."

' "No, Broad, not tonight, but we'll make it an extra big one tomorrow."

'We do. But that is another story. . . .'

The Hudson that attacked in the late afternoon of 28 May was from No 233 Squadron, based at Aldergrove in the valley just outside Belfast. The pilot reported sighting the destroyer *Tartar* firing its anti-aircraft guns at a He111 flying at about 6,000 feet three miles west of Slyne Head.

The Hudson went straight into the attack opening fire from 500 yards – no hits were observed – but the enemy rear-gunner replied. The Hudson closed and from 400 yards started scoring hits. The Heinkel then climbed into cloud but fifteen minutes later a second enemy aircraft was seen at 7,000 feet. The Hudson's front-gun ammunition had been exhausted by the first encounter so the pilot closed to attack from 200 yards. The Heinkel took evasive action with short plunging dives but the Hudson maintained formation and the rear-gunner fired at 550 yards and the enemy aircraft immediately burst into flames. Two of the crew baled out just before their aircraft disappeared into the sea, on fire – the whole action had taken only two minutes.

Help was on the way for the returning destroyers. Two more Hudsons were despatched from Aldergrove and another from Limavady to protect the force during the early evening, and another four Hudsons took off from Limavady at 2115 to relieve them. It was one of these latter, from No 224 Squadron, that attacked a He111 at 2235.

The pilot reported that he was on protective escort to three destroyers when he saw the Heinkel. He immediately attacked and drove it off, causing the pilot to jettison its bombs. The Hudson was then hit by machine-gun fire. Two bullets went through the nose, the side gun was knocked out of the gunner's hand, one bullet went through the pilots flying boot, another punctured an oil pipe and half the aerial was shot away.

It was nearly an hour later when a Hudson on the same patrol spotted another He111 manoeuvring to attack. The pilot chased the enemy which flew over the Irish coast, the Hudson's gunners fired over 400 rounds at the German aircraft but it was not seen to crash.

Sub-Lieutenant Ludovic Kennedy was not the only officer to appreciate the arrival of the Hudsons. The Commander-in-Chief, Western Approaches signalled: 'Will you please convey my warmest congratulations to the commanding officer of No 233 Squadron on his fine achievement today?'

The following day the Air Officer Commanding Coastal Command signalled to No 15 Group: 'I am very pleased with the excellent fighting spirit shown by your aircraft on protection duty yesterday.'

VII

U-boat captured

Before the outbreak of the Second World War the Germans vainly sought permission to establish air bases in Iceland, ostensibly for an air service between the two countries. Following the German occupation of Denmark in the spring of 1940, Iceland, which was a sovereign kingdom under the crown of Denmark, established direct diplomatic relations with Great Britain and the United States. In May 1940 British troops occupied the island to forestall a possible German invasion and air bases were quickly set up.

A year later United States naval forces landed with the permission of the Icelandic premier and also established bases.

Had the Germans been given permission to use the Icelandic bases or had they invaded the country the results would have been too terrible to contemplate; the combination of U-boats with air protection, or submarines and air attacks on Allied convoys would have put an entirely different face on the Battle of the Atlantic.

The Royal Air Force No 269 Hudson Squadron and a Norwegian squadron equipped with Northrop floatplanes were among the first aircraft to arrive and the former joined the ground forces on June 1941. Based at Kaldadarnes, they came under the command of No 15 Group from 13 July.

All towns and villages in Iceland were lit up at night and Reykjavik the capital, looked like fairyland. Most of the lighthouses along the coast were lit. Although there were listed emergency landing grounds all along the south coast there were many stretches of sand where a belly landing could safely be made, and some were good enough for a normal landing. The aircrews at Kaldadarnes lived mostly in Nissen huts and for recreation they fished for salmon or trout, shot duck, hacked on the white Icelandic ponies or attended the visiting ENSA concerts.

Iceland has a relatively mild and equable climate despite its high altitude and its proximity to the Arctic regions; however wind storms of considerable violence are characteristic and many Hudsons, although protected by wind-breaks built of lava and turf and securely staked to the ground, were damaged when their stakes broke due to the high winds. During the late spring and summer months there is practically no darkness.

Among the 269 Squadron personnel was James H. Thompson, a pre-war Reserve officer who held the rank of acting squadron leader. Like most of the Coastal Command pilots he had been flying long, boring, patrols since the early days of the war with little excitement to break the monotony. However, fate was soon to play into his hands and boost the morale of Hudson pilots all over the globe.

The Type VIIC U-boat was that most used by the German Navy throughout the war and *U-570* was one of these boats. The U-boat left Trondheim towards the end of August 1941 under the command of Hans Rahmlow, who together with his first officer had served in submarines since the beginning of the war. After leaving the Norwegian port the submarine followed a route just below the 64th parallel between the Faeroes and the south coast of Iceland, to patrol an area where U-boat Command believed three convoys were shortly due. Fully provisioned for a two month voyage *U-570* was to be the southernmost boat of a series of U-boats stationed strategically to intercept the expected convoys.

At 0640 on 27 August, the commander decided to submerge to 15 fathoms to avoid the heavy seas that had sharply reduced his U-boat's surface speed. The submarine surfaced briefly nearly an hour later and then dived again. At 1050 the U-boat resurfaced to make a routine radio report and before her crew knew what was happening they found themselves under attack from the air.

The attacking aircraft was Hudson S-Sugar, piloted by 32-year-old Yorkshireman James Thompson. It was not just good luck that the aircraft was in the right place, as earlier when Kapitänleutnant Rahmlow had first submerged, another Hudson of the same squadron had seen what the pilot described as 'the swirl and wake of a U-boat'. He immediately dropped smoke-floats to mark the position and signalled a first-sighting report back to base and circled the position. His patience was rewarded when at 0730 the submarine had briefly surfaced. The Hudson came in for an attack with depth charges but for some inexplicable reason they all hung-up. The frustrated pilot could only radio a second sighting report and call for reinforcements. Thus there was a second Hudson in the area when *U-570* came up to report.

At the time of the attack there was a rough sea with visibility down to two miles. The U-boat was sighted surfacing, at a range of 1,200 yards. The Hudson went straight in, the four 250 lb depth charge carried had been primed to explode at 50 feet. The pilot went down to 100 feet above the sea and released his depth charges in a stick with 60-foot spacings. By now the submarine was diving and was completely enveloped by the explosions, disappearing from sight. Two minutes later it shot to the surface and a dozen men came out of the conning-tower on to the deck. To prevent them manning their deck-gun the aircraft's wireless operator unwound the belly-gun, and as the Hudson approached again his tracers ripped down at the sleek hull. As the crew retreated back the navigator said: 'I've waited all my life to see those baskets scrambling out of a conning-tower!'

Several minutes later as the aircraft circled the stricken U-boat for the fifth time the Hudson's crew were amazed to see a white flag being waved from the conning-tower. A submarine surrendering to a land-based aircraft! The Hudson radioed a message back to base and requested help. The attack took place about eighty miles south of Iceland. Later in the day a Catalina flying-boat arrived from Northern Ireland to take over from the Hudson, who signalled before it left: 'Look after our – repeat OUR – submarine, which has flown the white flag.' It was twelve hours after the Hudson attacked before the first ship arrived, and the German crew in the U-boat had to wait until the next day for rescue.

One of the German officers told his rescuers:

We were bombed while surfacing to make signals. The attack damaged the bow ballast tank and we were unable to blow it, all the instruments were shattered, the batteries were sprung and sea water entered the boat, which was bow down to the sea. Gases from the battery permeated the compartments. There was just enough electricity generated to ventilate the boat and the crew mustered in the conning-tower preparatory to abandoning ship. On seeing the boat was still seaworthy several ratings returned below to estimate the damage. At this time the aircraft overhead machine-gunned us but ceased when we hoisted a white flag. There was an extremely rough sea and the U-boat was making water, but there was enough electricity for the pumps.

The officer then went on to describe the rest of the day:

Later a flying-boat arrived on the scene and remained until it was dark at about 2300 when the first trawler arrived on the scene. We did not attempt to abandon ship because of the darkness and the rough sea. We lightened ship by discharging ammunition and provisions but were unable to touch our torpedoes because of the inability to approach the tubes.

At daylight more ships and aircraft arrived and later the submarine crew were taken off. Another German officer told his rescuers that the U-boat had only commissioned six months earlier and the sole cause of surrender was the smashing of every instrument by the explosions from the depth charges. A young German watch-keeping officer added that the depth charges also caused a leak and badly shook all on board.

The next day a boarding party made an inspection of the submarine and attempts were made to open the door between the control room and the petty officers' mess but as chlorine gas was detected the door was immediately closed. The for'ard bulkhead of the after battery tank was found to be buckled as a result of a pressure wave from the explosion of the depth charges passing up through the open Kingstons of the Number 3 main ballast tank and being transmitted through the fuel in the internal oil fuel tank of which this bulkhead formed a part. This caused severe damage to the cells in the vicinity.

Eventually, after a great deal of hard work and good seamanship by the Royal Navy, the U-boat was towed to Iceland where she was beached – this caused more damage. When she finally arrived in Britain, the conclusion reached after full inspection was :

It would appear that the Germans surrendered their ship under the impression that she was more badly damaged than she in fact was. The fact that all the lights went out, the main and auxiliary motors stopped, and water rushed into several compartments may well have caused a most discreditable panic. It is however very difficult to understand why, when the crew had at least four hours of lying on the surface guarded only by one Hudson aircraft which was then armed only with machine guns, no attempt was made to assess the actual damage, repair it, dive and escape.

On board the submarine the German crew had done their best to

No 269 Squadron Hudsons over Iceland.

destroy instruments so that they would be of no use to the Allies. The sabotage was chiefly in the wireless room where many valves were smashed as well as panels of the sets. The attack instrument in the conning tower was defaced and damaged. The forward periscope was lowered into its well and filled with water and oil and a binocular attachment on this periscope was removed and thrown overboard. However, no scuttling charges were placed. At the time of the surrender the captain and crew probably thought the submarine would eventually sink and her secrets with her, and that if she did not, the damage they had done would ensure that the Allies did not benefit from her capture.

After the war one German admiral was to record that the capture of *U-570* had serious consequences for the U-boat campaign, for the British discovered much that was helpful to anti-submarine operations – the volume and character of the U-boat's various machinery noises, its manoeuvering characteristics and its diving capacity. For these trials the *U-570* was commissioned into the Royal Navy and named HMS *Graph*.

The capture of *U-570* was only the first round for the Hudson and it deservedly won a Distinguished Flying Cross for the pilot and navigator.

VIII

Far-Eastern Air War

In mid-1940 when the Battle of Britain was at its height the Prime Minister of Australia suggested that perhaps the RAAF could lighten the load of the RAF by taking over some of its responsibilities in Malaya. The offer was gratefully accepted.

By July 1941 two Hudson squadrons Nos 1 and 8 RAAF whose primary task was seaward reconnaissance and attacks on enemy sea-borne forces, with operations as light bombers as a secondary role, had been in Malaya long enough to be regarded as seasoned. Because, in so small a force, specialisation was impracticable, the Hudson crews together with the RAF Blenheims had to be trained for both day and night bombing. The probable targets in Indo-China were only just within range of these aircraft but since sea-borne invasion was the main threat to Malaya the Hudsons were needed for the vital seaward reconnaissance.

In the same month, the Vichy French regime signed a pact with Japan giving the Japanese use of eight airfields in Indo-China. It became obvious that war was imminent as the Japanese had built up their air strength in Indo-China from 74 to 245 aircraft in two months and information was received that part of the Japanese fleet was in the South China sea.

In Malaya second degree readiness was ordered on the first day of December. No 1 Squadron RAAF was at Kota Bharu and No 8 Squadron RAAF moved up to Sembawang, but their advance party of eight Hudsons did not arrive there until 4 December. The monsoon weather then grounded all aircraft for 48 hours. On 6 December three Hudsons managed to get off the rain-soaked runway at Kota Bharu to search the three sectors allotted to the unit. Less than two hours after take-off, the pilot of one of the Hudsons reported seeing a Japanese motor ship, minelayer and a minesweeper about 185 miles from base. A quarter-of-an-hour later he reported seeing a battleship, five cruisers, seven destroyers and 22 transports, these were a further 80 miles to the east but steering due west. A float-plane was seen to take off from the force and the Hudson took to the clouds to report the sighting. A second Hudson later also reported the force.

The fateful day – 7 December 1941 – dawned with rain and low clouds, but despite this three Hudsons were ordered off at first light from No 1 Squadron; they failed to sight anything significant. It was mid-afternoon when a Hudson from No 8 Squadron sighted a Japanese merchant ship steaming south with 'a large number of men on deck in khaki'. At this news more Hudsons took off and sighted a small force which included a cruiser that opened fire on the aircraft. Those in command in Malaya at the time were inclined to think that the heavily escorted convoy was about to launch an attack on Thailand. Just before midnight local time the Japanese struck. In the space of fourteen hours Malaya, Hawaii, Thailand, the Philippines, Guam, Hongkong and Wake Island had all been attacked.

The coastal defence force in Malaya reported seeing some small vessels near the coast just after midnight. Six Hudsons were ordered off, the first aircraft officially to take up the air war against Japanese forces.

Soon after 0200 the Hudsons took off in quick succession with orders to attack independently any hostile forces seen. The aircraft carried four 250 lb bombs each with an 11-second delay fuse. In the first attack on three transports a Hudson missed with the first two bombs and was heavily engaged by the ships, returned and bombed again. One of the bombs hit a transport amidships. One Hudson failed to return and many were holed by anti-aircraft fire. The Hudsons were keeping up their reputation of mast-height attackers.

Interrogation of the crews showed that there were probably three cruisers and as many destroyers and transports with several barges. Ten more sorties were carried out against the transports and landing ships taking troops from the convoy to the shore. Several vessels were overturned but another Hudson failed to return.

At 0330 a further reconnaissance was made by a Hudson thirty miles seawards from Kota Bharu and a cruiser and three destroyers were seen, the pilot reported when he arrived back at base:

Seeing a ship underneath me about ten miles from the coast I decided to attack. It was a nice moonlight night and going out wide I came in at sea level for a mast-height attack. When within half-a-mile of this ship it put up such a concentrated ack-ack barrage that I realised it was a cruiser and veered off around its bows taking violent avoiding action while my rear gunner machine-gunned the decks as we passed. Realising the mistake I had made in attempting to attack a cruiser from low level, I returned towards the merchant ship near the beach and carried out an attack on the vessel which was stationed about four miles out apparently unloading troops, as it was surrounded by barges. I encountered considerable light ack-ack fire during my bombing run, but took violent avoiding action and dropped my stick of four bombs across its bows, getting a direct hit. It is possible that my other bombs did considerable damage to the barges which were clustered round the sides of the vessel, but it was too dark to say definitely. There was considerable barge activity and no scarcity of targets, which we machine-gunned as opportunity offered while returning to the aerodrome.

Hudsons at this stage of the war mounted two fixed Browning .303 inch guns in the nose, two in the rear power turret and two side guns. The side guns were unorthodox: a field modification in which they were mounted inside the aircraft, with the muzzles protruding through an opening out in the perspex of a window to give a useful though restricted field of fire.

In an attack on the transports by another aircraft a direct hit was scored just for'ard of the bridge; the gunners swept the vessel's decks with their fire and as the aircraft turned away the ship could be seen burning from the bomb burst. Most of the heavy anti-aircraft fire came from a cruiser lying about half-a-mile to seaward of the transport. This Hudson returned to base with one engine out of service and holes in the wings, fuselage and tailplane.

Another attack by Hudsons blew up one of the transports and overturned twenty-four barges. So great was the explosion of the ship blowing up that those at the base on shore heard it. There was one slight mystery when the RAAF crews reported that the Japanese ships gave the correct recognition signal of the day for Allied forces!

The aircraft returned to base to refuel and rearm. At 0600 one was airborne again to see the effect of the night's attacks. The reconnaissance showed that one large transport was alight three miles from shore and further out to sea a force of two cruisers, four destroyers and two merchant ships including the landing-craft carrier were retreating at high speed protected by a formation of Japanese aircraft – the first seen since the beginning of hostilities.

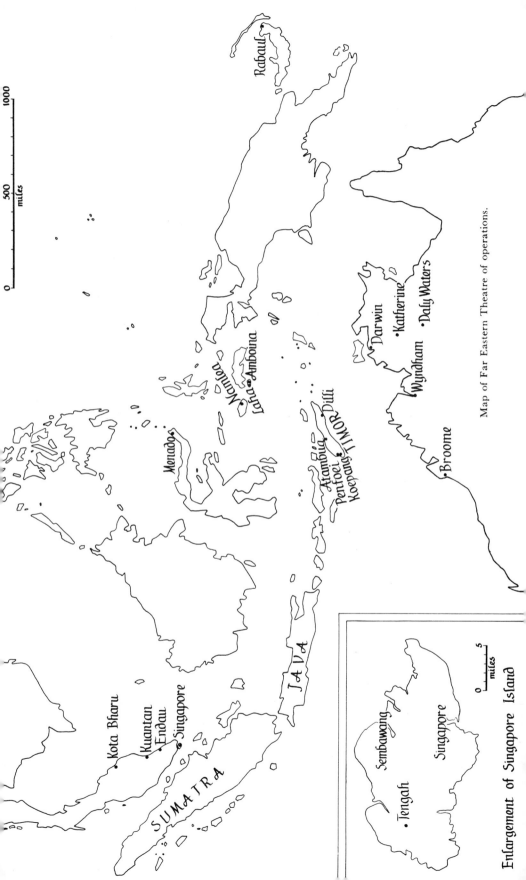

1000

500

0

miles

Rabaul

Darwin
Katherine
Daly Waters
Wyndham
Broome

Map of Far Eastern Theatre of operations.

Manado
Namlea
Laha Amboina

Atamboea
Penfoei
Koepang TIMOR Dilli

Kota Bharu
Kuantan
Endau
Singapore

SUMATRA

JAVA

Sembawang
Tengah
Singapore

0   5
miles

Enlargement of Singapore Island

At dawn 8 Squadron flew off three flights of Hudsons and some Blenheims of 60 Squadron RAF took off in heavy fog and flew to the scene of the Japanese landing. Here the merchant ship that was already ablaze was again attacked as were several smaller vessels. One flight ordered to attack the retreating sea force were unable to find it due to heavy rain. Two of the Hudsons were so badly damaged that they had to force land. One Hudson reported shooting down an enemy fighter in the sea.

The Japanese transport that was on fire and later sank was the 9,700-ton *Awagosam Maru*. This was the first Japanese ship sunk in the war against Japan; all told she suffered ten direct hits.

Meanwhile almost the entire strength of No 1 Squadron Hudsons had been concentrated on the enemy's landing operations; some were attacked by Japanese Zero fighters. Reconnaissance photographs showed that the Japanese had sixty aircraft on the Thailand Singora airfield and it was soon after that the Japanese air force made their first attack on the Kota Bharu airfield. The bombers and fighters attacked at very low level showing great determination, but nevertheless the Hudsons were able to continue their sorties. Later in the day the Japanese land forces penetrated close to the airfield and two Hudsons were lost with their crews. Aircraft damaged were cannibalised from others in order to keep as many as possible flying; in fact by mid-afternoon only five aircraft were airworthy.

In the early evening an order was received that all possible aircraft were to be flown to Kuantan and after demolition the airfield at Kota Bharu was to be evacuated. The five serviceable Hudsons took off loaded with 700 pounds of equipment in each. Three Hudsons that could not be repaired in time were destroyed.

There was some drama in the evacuation. One of the Hudsons was so badly damaged that the wing flaps would not remain in the up position and the undercarriage would not retract. The flaps were tied into position with wire and the aircraft flew wheels down to Kuantan where a safe landing was achieved at dusk. Another damaged Hudson had seventeen passengers aboard and was attacked by small arms fire as soon as it took off; this fire was returned by the rear gunner. The same aircraft managed to evade no fewer than six Japanese Zeros by flying almost on the deck, and landed safely.

While Kota Bharu was being evacuated Singapore experienced its first air raid of the war. Elsewhere the Japanese were also making their presence felt – not least in that most infamous of attacks on Pearl Harbor in Hawaii.

On 10 December the Japanese had one of the biggest successes of the Second World War when their aircraft sank HMS *Prince of Wales* and HMS *Repulse* which had now arrived off the coast of Malaya with a destroyer escort but unescorted by any air protection. The explosions from the sinking warships were heard on the airfield at Kuantan – where fighters took off from the airfield, not knowing of the presence of the Allied ships due to secrecy. All they saw was the rescue operation being carried out by the escorting destroyers. The sinking of the two large Royal Naval ships had cost the Japanese only four bombers.

The next day Air Headquarters, anxious about the concentration of aircraft at Kuantan, ordered all but twelve Vildebeestes and the thirteen surviving Hudsons of the two Australian squadrons to return at once to Singapore. In the early part of the day three Hudsons of No 8 Squadron made a parallel track search to seaward but within sight of the coast. The pilot reported a convoy which he listed as two cruisers, seven destroyers and three transports. As preparations were being made to attack these ships, nine Japanese aircraft bombed the airfield. One Hudson already in the air intercepted the Japanese bombers and claimed one enemy aircraft destroyed. The Japanese completed their bombing however and later machine-gunned the airfield. Later in the day the seven remaining airworthy Hudsons flew further back, this time to Sembawang.

When a count was taken at Sembawang on Christmas Eve, No 1 and No 8 RAAF Squadrons were found to have only five and eight serviceable Hudsons respectively. These Hudsons with the aid of Catalinas of 205 Squadron RAF were responsible for long sea reconnaissance flights and these long flights were overtaxing the aircraft – at one time the two squadrons had only six serviceable aircraft between them. Help was coming, however, and on Christmas Day eight replacement Hudsons arrived from Australia. The two Hudson squadrons were then given the task of patrolling the South China Sea.

On 15 January six Hudsons from No 8 Squadron were despatched to search for a convoy of small ships reported off the Malayan coast but they were unable to find them. Three days later three escorted Hudsons were again unable to find a reported ship but this time they were attacked by Japanese Zero fighters. One of the Hudsons

A RAAF Hudson showing its clean cut distinctive lines.

was chased for about twenty miles among the surrounding hills until a Buffalo of the escort succeeded in diverting and possibly shooting down one of the two pursuing Zeros before rejoining the Hudson and escorting it safely back to Sembawang. The other two Hudsons had turned seaward with at least five Zeros in pursuit. The rudder control of one was damaged by enemy fire so the pilot of the other flew his aircraft as escort. The formation crossed the north of Sumatra before the damaged aircraft could be turned round. In late afternoon, as both Hudsons were approaching to land, the damaged aircraft went into a spin and crashed on the edge of the airfield bursting into flames.

In southern Malaya the land troops met the same problem that they had faced in central Malaya, but in even more acute form: the defence of a string of airfields and landing grounds was urgent if the enemy was to be prevented from doubling the scale of his attacks on the Singapore area and on incoming convoys. Yet effective strength to prevent him from doing so simply did not exist and the situation in Malaya steadily worsened.

Early on the morning of the 26th two Hudsons left Sembawang on reconnaissance up the east coast looking for enemy ships that had been reported the previous day. They found two cruisers, twelve destroyers, two 10,000 ton transports and three barges about ten miles from, and steaming towards, Endau about ninety miles north of Singapore. Enemy radio interference with communications prevented them from transmitting the news to Air Headquarters at Singapore. Meanwhile three enemy fighters attacked the Hudsons, whose gunners, however, scored hits which probably destroyed two of them. Using cloud cover, the pilots succeeded in evading further combat and returned to Sembawang to report that the enemy was almost certainly about to land a strong force. An immediate air attack was ordered but the total striking force available to Far East Command now consisted of only nine Hudsons (from Nos 1 and 8 Squadrons) twenty-one obsolete Vildebeestes and three Albacores. There was also some difficulty raising sufficient fighters to protect the bombers and the first force, of Vildebeestes, did not get off until after midday. An hour later the nine Hudsons joined the fray. By this time the enemy landings were well advanced. Five of the dozen Vildebeestes were shot down by enemy fighters and as the remainder turned for base the Hudsons bore the brunt of the enemy attack. One Hudson pilot recorded:

Unarmed Hudson with cabin sun-blind pulled, possibly the squadron hack.

No 13 Squadron ground crews loading up a Hudson.

We were no sooner in sight of the Japanese ships, when some fifty Zeros jumped on us from above. I was flying in the centre of the closely packed formation of nine aircraft and the first Zero attacked from above. With his first burst he killed my wireless operator, who was on one of the side guns, and also killed my second pilot who was sitting alongside me. The second pilot was killed by a bullet through the head, which afterwards struck me on the shoulder, knocking me over the controls, and lodging underneath the badges of rank on my shirt. The bullet when it struck me was apparently almost spent. We were at 7,000 feet when attacked, and the next thing I remembered was diving, almost vertically through clouds. I pulled out of the dive and remained in the cloud as I took stock of what had happened. I tried to call my rear-gunner on the intercom but it had been shot away during the attack, and I was unable to find out if he was alive. My second pilot's feet were all tangled up amongst the throttle and bomb door levers, and I was unable to control the aircraft and lift him out of the way at the same time. I could not get my bomb doors open for bombing so I decided to return to base. The cloud cover was big lumpy cumulus from 2-7,000 feet, and was about 7/10 covered. The enemy fighters were playing a game of hide-and-seek tactics with the Hudsons. They would cruise around above the ground waiting for the Hudsons to come out and then shoot them up. After several attempts I made my way from cloud to cloud and eventually got out of the area.

Another pilot of No 1 Squadron sighted a motor vessel through a break in the cloud, put his aircraft into a dive, and obtained two direct hits and two near misses with his four bombs. Enemy fighters prevented further observation of the results of this attack. The other Hudsons attacked ships and troop concentrations ashore. All the bombers succeeded in getting back to Sembawang as did all the Buffalo fighters. Of the nine Vildebeestes and three Albacores, six were shot down and the others were all damaged by gunfire.

In attempting to land at dusk at Singapore two of the Hudsons crashed near the naval base. The wireless operator of one of them sent out a signal just before crashing reporting that the rear-gunner had shot down at least two enemy aircraft. The other four aircraft landed safely at Tengah. Belated and understrength though it had been, the attack had resulted in direct hits on both transports and one cruiser and two destroyers although later it was found that there were no actual sinkings. Thirteen enemy aircraft were claimed shot down but this did not compensate for the eighteen Allied aircraft lost, the majority with their crews.

On the same day the commander in Malaya was given permission to withdraw his troops to Singapore Island at his discretion – and withdrawal began four days later. Singapore now became congested and it was inevitable that it was only a matter of time before regular attacks from the air could be expected. It was imperative that all aircraft not required for the local defence of the island be evacuated. In these circumstances Air Headquarters had no alternative to progressive withdrawal of most of its squadrons to the Netherlands East Indies. On 27 January 1942 No 8 Squadron's aircrews were flown to Sumatra. No 1 Squadron took over the 14 Hudsons that No 8 had left at Sembawang, but only five of these were airworthy. No 1 Squadron now had sixteen serviceable aircraft and with these the vital reconnaissance flights were continued. For two days a chain reconnaissance was carried out; this consisted of Hudsons taking off at two-hour intervals from dawn to dusk to patrol from Johore to the Natuna Islands. But, by the end of the month, apart from a few Hudson sorties for convoy protection, air operations from Singapore were almost entirely confined to those by the Hurricanes in their vain effort to defend the island.

On 10 February there was a complete air force withdrawal from Singapore. In a last and desperate effort to deprive the enemy of as much advantage as possible, airfield surfaces were ploughed up, and petrol and equipment stores demolished. Singapore surrendered on 15 February 1942.

After the fighting had finished in Malaya and Singapore, the Allies were pushed right back almost to Australia. All this time the Hudson was playing its part in the front-line.

Towards the end of January 1942 the Japanese occupied Rabaul. There were only two Wirraway fighters and a Hudson to evacuate airmen, some of whom were wounded. The Hudson took off at 0300 one morning, filled with wounded men. Two or three lights were placed at the far end of the runway, and just after the Hudson became airborne one engine faltered, it picked up again and after four hours reached Port Moresby. Here the aircraft was refuelled and set out for Australia. When halfway to its destination, and over

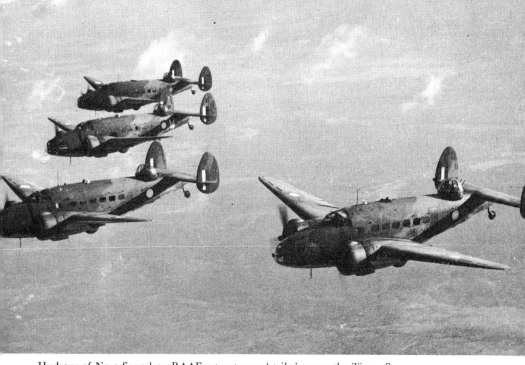

Hudsons of No 2 Squadron RAAF set out on a 'strike' across the Timor Sea.

Ground crew swarm round as the No 2 Squadron Hudson receives its 60 hour inspection at Hughes Field, Northern Territory.

the sea, the faulty engine packed up altogether, so all guns, ammunition and anything portable were jettisoned and the pilot just reached Australia on one engine.

Ammunition and guns were again discarded when a Japanese invading force was seen making for Ambon. The Hudsons here were stripped on the ground, given a minimal amount of petrol; thus the overall weight was drastically reduced so that the aircraft could evacuate the maximum number of men. In one aircraft there were 23 men aboard! One of them recorded the journey thus:

> It took the whole length of the runway to get off. There was no flare path and only a pale moon to guide the pilot. All passengers stood for the whole journey, parked between the pilot and the second main spar of the aircraft – only one man was aft of that, the air gunner. The journey took four and a half hours and we were glad to be relieved from our cramped positions; we were so crushed that we couldn't lift our arms.

Two other Hudsons that took off at the same time evacuated fifteen and twenty-two men, the first aircraft had already been damaged before leaving the ground.

At the beginning of February a Hudson based on Port Moresby took off for New Britain on reconnaissance. The Hudson was piloted by the squadron's navigating officer, who was filling in because many of the pilots were showing signs of operational fatigue. Over Rabaul the Hudson crew saw an enemy fighter take off and four minutes later this aircraft engaged them in combat at 10,000 feet. It made two attacks, breaking off the fight after having riddled the Hudson with bullet holes. An explosive bullet had shattered the pilot's left wrist and severed the little finger. The second pilot was seriously wounded; his left arm and leg were fractured and his right hand injured. The turret gunner who had fired 100 rounds on to the enemy aircraft at a range of about a hundred yards was severely wounded in the left leg. The fourth member of the crew was the only one not wounded and he gave first aid to his fellow crew members and then assisted the pilot to fly the aircraft. This had to be done without either altimeter or airspeed indicator, both of which had been smashed by bullets. The enemy fighter's gunfire had also hit the sea markers carried in the Hudson, exploding them so that the aircraft was filled with a dense cloud of fine aluminium powder.

The top two Hudsons have the Boulton Paul turret and the lower one a covered dorsal turret mounting only.

No 2 Squadron bomb up a Hudson.

Enduring the pain from his wounds and loss of blood, the pilot guided the Hudson throughout its 500-mile flight back to base, in bad weather. When close to Port Moresby one of the self-sealing fuel tanks, which had been damaged by gunfire, opened up as the aircraft was brought down to make a landing. Just as the pilot began the approach to the runway both engines failed. The unwounded crew member, with great presence of mind, operated the auxiliary fuel or 'wobble' pump in time to revive them and allow the pilot to put the Hudson down safely on the runway. When the ground crew took the aircraft over for servicing and repair they found only five gallons of fuel left in the tanks.

Five days later, during which time there had been reconnaissance and bombing attacks on enemy sea forces, three Hudsons made the first mast-height attack on enemy shipping in the New Guinea campaign. One of the crews put four bombs across one transport directly amidships, another made a direct hit amidships on a second transport, while the third aircraft made a low-level sweep over the first transport using incendiary ammunition which set the ship on fire. Both ships were enveloped in clouds of black smoke. As the Hudsons climbed away they were intercepted by five or six enemy fighters. One of the Hudsons, with one engine on fire and enemy aircraft pursuing it, dived steeply into a hillside killing all the crew. The leader of the Hudsons was just bringing his plane out from the attack when his second pilot reported that it was on fire. The pilot took evasive action to throw off an enemy fighter and the second pilot broke a window and tried to put the flames out with a hand extinguisher. When this failed and the intensity of the fire increased, the pilot ordered the crew to abandon the aircraft. They moved to the rear door to bale out. As the flames reached the cockpit, the pilot, using the control column as a step, climbed up and tried to force himself through the window. The Hudson went into a dive so he pulled the column back with his feet, kicked the trimming tab and, as the aircraft climbed again, pushed his way through the window and baled out. In landing he fell into a tree and was suspended above the ground by his parachute with his 'Mae West' life-jacket almost choking him, but he succeeded in getting free by pulling himself up into the branches of the tree. He arrived back at base nine days after he had been officially posted as missing.

On a sortie later in the month a Hudson was attacked by two fighters. The tail gunner, after firing two thousand rounds, saw one of the attacking aircraft diving out of control. In this combat the wireless operator was fatally wounded and died on the return flight. The turret gunner returned with a spent bullet in one of his flying boots. One tyre on the Hudson's undercarriage had been punctured, a portion of the flap cable severed and the airframe, turret and propellers had been perforated by bullets, but the pilot brought it back and made a safe landing.

All this time the Japanese were attacking further south and nearing Australia. It became obvious that an invasion of Sumatra could not be long delayed, although by now the Japanese were stretching their lines of communication and supplies to a dangerous level. Although as the Allies withdrew nearer to Australia they would become better equipped for the defence of the country, temporarily they were reduced to a token force after being continually in air battles with the Japanese. The remaining crews were still determined and full of initiative and this was fully illustrated when a Hudson escaped from two Japanese Navy Zeros. The aircraft had its starboard engine put out of action, its starboard wheel shot away and its tail plane seriously damaged. But with full throttle on the one serviceable engine the pilot flew the Hudson at a height of only a hundred feet and succeeded in reaching an aerodrome where he made a crash landing without injury to his crew or himself. Finding the aerodrome infested by Japanese paratroopers, he led his crew to a Hudson standing on the runway; unfortunately this aircraft had already been abandoned as the tips were missing from its propeller blades. The pilot tried but failed to get this aircraft off the ground; with its damaged propellers the best speed he could get was only 40 knots. However, the aircrew escaped pursued by the enemy and reached Allied forces safely.

One of the No 1 Squadron Hudsons had an adventurous journey at this time delivering evacuation orders. Finding that his destination was occupied by the Japanese, the pilot put down at a nearby airfield to refuel for the return journey. The facilities were meagre and the crew had to use cans without even the benefit of a chamois leather filter. The result of this was that when the aircraft was approaching the coast of Java both engines stopped almost simultaneously because there was water in the fuel. The pilot prepared to make a crash landing and at the same time switched the fuel feed over to a tank that had not been topped up. As the Hudson was about to come down both engines picked up enough to enable the aircraft to climb again and continue flying. After a further forced landing the fuel system was drained and replenished before continuing a journey that had occupied 15 hours' flying time.

The Allies lost the sea battle of the Java Sea and the Japanese invaded Java on 1 March 1942. Plans were made to send as many Hudsons as possible back to Australia. The crews had been experimenting with an ingenious method of in-flight refuelling from petrol tins. Each aircraft carried an additional 100 gallons of petrol in four-gallon tins. Refuelling was done by knocking out a side window and reaching out and opening a wing tank. A length of rubber tubing was thrust into the tank and petrol was poured out of the tins through a strainer and funnel down the tubing and into the tank.

The Japanese completed their invasion of Java just a week after landing and Australia's northern coastline was now only a few hundred miles of sea away from them.

While Nos 1 and 8 Squadrons were in Malaya and making a gradual return to Australia, Nos 2 and 13 Squadrons were much nearer home. In June 1940 No 2 Squadron RAAF was re-equipped with Hudsons. In October 1941 four Hudsons were flown to Darwin and made highly successful reconnaissances of the Netherlands East Indies bases at Laha, Namlea and Koepang. Little did the men know that the names of those towns would mean so much to them in the months to come.

Because of the obviously possibility of war the unit was ordered to stand by to move from Laverton to Darwin at short notice. At the time the squadron consisted of twelve Hudsons, and these were moved to the Northern Territory between 5 and 7 December. This fateful week saw the actual outbreak of the struggle with Japan, and almost immediately No 2 Squadron moved again, this time to Koepang, in Dutch Timor. From there it drew its first blood from the enemy when some of its aircraft attacked the Japanese ship *Nanyo Maru* off the north coast of Timor. The ship was damaged, went aground on a small island and was abandoned by the crew who were interned.

By 10 December the whole of No 2 Squadron was based at Koepang; from here the unit operated under extremely difficult and trying conditions, for life there was almost insupportably stark and bare. The RAAF base at Penfoei, near Koepang, had been occupied for some months prior to the arrival of the squadron, but only by a skeleton staff. Barracks, Operations Room and W/T installations were practically completed, but there were no anti-aircraft defences, camouflaged areas or shelter pens at the base. As the squadron maintenance flight was stationed at Darwin, all aircraft had to proceed to that town for maintenance and repairs, a situation which added considerably to the difficulties of the unit. All aircraft and essential ground staff were located at Koepang.

One of the first duties on Timor was the provision of anti-submarine patrols and air cover for the 2/40th Battalion, Australian Infantry Force, in their move from Darwin. Besides the AIF there were also 300 native and Dutch troops in Timor. The troops were established in barracks adjacent to Penfoei airfield, and began immediately to prepare defensive positions in the vicinity of the strip, on the beaches, near the town and at Klapalima.

The intensity of Japanese submarine activity in this period eventually forced those in charge of the Allied forces to decide to occupy the Portuguese portion of Timor. As the Portuguese were obviously unable and in fact unwilling to defend their own colony, the Australian and Dutch commanders in Timor sent an ultimatum to the Portuguese Governor, who replied that although he could naturally not agree to its terms, he could not, on the other hand, actively resist the occupation. Accordingly, a force of approximately 500 Dutch and native troops and an independent company of the 2/40th Battalion proceeded to Dilli by sea and occupied the town and airfield without opposition. No 2 Squadron Hudsons provided anti-submarine patrols and air cover for this force. The Portuguese Governor, officials and a majority of the population retired to the hills.

In the meantime, preparations for the defence of Penfoei and Koepang were going ahead. Slit trenches were dug and efforts were made to prepare dispersal areas and aircraft shelter pens. By the close of the year, emergency landing grounds had been prepared at Mina River, about forty miles from Koepang, and the squadron was once again in a comparatively strong and defended position. At the close of the year, too 'A' Flight of No 2 Squadron moved to Namlea.

The squadron continued with its effective anti-submarine patrols, and besides this, frequent raids were made on Menado, in the Celebes, where a quantity of enemy shipping was damaged. No 2 Squadron received close support from No 13 Squadron RAAF, also equipped with Hudsons. These two squadrons bore for most of 1942 the whole

(*Left*) Training the belly gun of a Hudson V. (*Below*) Remarkable picture showing the ventral turret of a No 13 Squadron Hudson retracted while in action over New Guinea in late 1942.

brunt of the Japanese onrush through the Dutch archipelago, for they constituted the main part of Australia's striking force in the air.

As the battle raged more and more fiercely, No 2 Squadron's flight at Namlea was reinforced and continued to carry out bombing and reconnaissance work against the enemy forces which had occupied Menado. Namlea and Amboina were subjected to frequent air attacks and some aircraft were destroyed on the ground. Then a large enemy convoy was seen to be approaching the area. For reasons of strategical expediency, Namlea and Amboina were evacuated. This did not deter the remainder of the squadron at Koepang from making every effort to defend their posts. To avoid destruction on the ground, all Hudsons were moved to the emergency landing ground and camouflaged in the surrounding jungle. By February, all aircraft and aircrews of No 2 Squadron were based on Darwin and were under the operational control of the Commanding Officer of No 13 Squadron.

On 19 February, the day that No 2 Squadron moved to Darwin, the RAAF station there was raided by a large formation of enemy aircraft. This raid was a serious setback, for the unit lost four Hudsons on the ground, the squadron headquarters were totally destroyed, and all unit records and publications disappeared. However, there were no casualties in the squadron and indeed they did not stay out of the battle for long. Before many weeks had elapsed, they were making successful raids on Dilli and Koepang, as well as reconnaissances over the Timor area.

On 8 March the Japanese had landed at Salamaua and Lae. RAAF bombers attacked the enemy troopships with some success in the face of fierce opposition. Two days later, American pilots appeared in Australian skies for the first time when RAAF and US Navy aircraft bombed shipping at Lae and Salamaua.

On 30 April the RAAF became a component of the Allied Air Force, an organisation which consolidated all US, RAAF, RAF and Dutch service squadrons in the SW Pacific area.

The first serious set-back encountered by the enemy in his rush southwards was the Battle of the Coral Sea early in May 1942. Towards the end of April the enemy at Rabaul gathered vast forces for a sea assault on Port Moresby, but Allied naval and air power were already too strong, and the Japanese were repulsed after a bitter three-day battle.

RAAF Hudsons and Catalinas made reconnaissance flights over

the seas where the Japanese ships were located, supplying invaluable information to the American aircraft carriers. Heavy attacks on Japanese air bases in New Guinea and New Britain prevented the Japanese using their landbased aircraft in the battle. This was the turning of the tide.

On 13 May nine Hudsons set out from Darwin with the object of making a concentrated attack on enemy shipping, water tanks, power houses and wharves in the Ambon area. The aircraft took off before dawn, and did not return for almost ten hours, in which time they inflicted considerable damage on the enemy. Five of the aircraft crossed the coast of Ambon south-east of the town, skimming over the tops of the hills behind it. Past the hills the formation opened out, each aircraft taking a different ship and attacking it from mast-head height with four general purpose bombs of 250 lb. fitted with eleven-second delay fuses. Immediately following these, three aircraft came in from the east at 1,000 feet and released five semi-armour-piercing bombs of the same weight. The attack was a complete surprise, and no anti-aircraft fire was met until the first flight was already on its way down the bay. Some firing came from a destroyer and merchant vessels, but no enemy aircraft was encountered during the attack.

Tragedy followed in the wake when a Hudson made its attack on a 3,000-ton ship from mast-head height; the ship blew up and the aircraft was seen to explode in mid-air at the same time. The result of the strike was that one ship was sunk, two badly damaged and another near missed. In addition a fire was left burning on the coal wharf.

Later a plan was made for three Hudsons to make an attack on shipping in Dilli harbour. These aircraft all left base in formation, but, owing to a faulty port engine which finally righted itself, the aircraft piloted by Pilot Officer James lost formation, was unable to pick up the other two and arrived over the target four minutes after the others had released their bombs. When the first two arrived over Dilli, nothing was to be seen in the harbour, so Flight Lieutenant Hay proceeded over the airfield, losing height to 3,000 feet and releasing his bombs. The second aircraft released its bombs over the town-ship.

While the third, late arrival, Hudson was leaving Dilli in a northerly direction over the sea, two Zeros were seen to take off. These aircraft made fierce attacks while James looked for cover amongst the clouds, beating the enemy off all the time. Two more Zeros then dived from the clouds. After fifteen rounds, the Hudson's port turret gun became unserviceable, but the aircraft continued to fight. Evasive tactics were used, stall turning being the main method of confusing the enemy. When one Zero made a belly attack, the Hudson's tunnel gunner was given his first real opportunity of driving home the attack on the enemy, the smoking Zero was sent down in a spin. Five minutes later another Zero which attempted to close in on the port beam of the Hudson, evidently with the aim of making an attack on the front of the aircraft, was raked with fire from the Hudson's turret gun. The Zero pulled up to 150 feet above the Hudson then spun earthwards with smoke trailing from it.

By this time the Hudson was over Witan Island, with the main wing tanks practically empty, the belly and side guns out of ammunition, and, a few minutes later, the turret unserviceable. Pilot Officer James then dived towards the water on a southerly course, levelling out several feet above sea level, the side gunner meanwhile taking 100 rounds from the front guns. The aircraft zigzagged across Witan Strait, the side gunner using short bursts of fire to ward off attacks from the stern quarter. His gun had become serviceable again, and he fired a short burst of ammunition into a Zero which was attacking from the starboard quarter – the Zero broke off the attack and headed towards Dilli.

This left only one enemy fighter. On reaching the coast of Timor the Hudson flew along valleys, very close to the ground, thereby making it impossible for the remaining Zero to attack from anywhere but the rear. The turret gunner was compelled to load the port gun by hand, with the result that he tore most of the skin off his hands in the process. Eventually this Zero, too, was shaken off, and the damaged but victorious Hudson limped back through the skies to Darwin. In the words of the squadron diarist, 'this being the first strike by this crew, it is considered a particularly good show. Pilot Officer James excelled in air tactics and the turret and tunnel gunners showed coolness under constant attack.' Damage to the Hudson consisted of only seventeen bullet holes.

Throughout this and the following year, No 2 Squadron, still armed with Hudson aircraft continued to perform its duties of bombing, strafing, making reconnaissances, escorting convoys and dropping supplies to outlying bases. Heavy damage was inflicted on both shipping and land installations.

Indian Hudson, the crew enjoy a cup of tea from the Cha-wallah in late 1943.

South African Air Force Hudson, on assembly at Capetown in May 1941. Two
had been swopped for Ansons by the RAF six months earlier.

An RAF squadron was formed in India to transport men and supplies through the length and breadth of Indian Command. In the first ten months the squadron set up a remarkable record by flying 1,440,000 miles from Lahore in the North to Ceylon in the South and from Calcutta in the East to Bombay in the West. Supplies were dropped in Burma. The squadron maintained a ferry service for the Army, Navy and Air Force throughout India and Ceylon.

Chinese Hudson. One of the lease-lend A-29's helping General Chiang Kai-Shek in the battle against the Japanese.

In November 1943 Flying Officer Michael Helsham won a DFC for his action in bringing back his Hudson after it had been hit by anti-aircraft fire. As the pilot was making a bombing run on Langgoer during a night raid, the controls of his aircraft were damaged, one petrol tank was punctured and the wireless ruined. The first decision of the captain was for the crew to bail out, but they stuck to their posts, and with superb skill and airmanship, Helsham managed to regain partial control of his aircraft. He flew it back over 400 miles of sea and made a smooth and successful crash-landing at his base without injury to the crew.

A fine tribute was paid to the Hudson pilots of No 2 Squadron by their one-time Commanding Officer Wing Commander John M. Whyte. At the end of his tour of duties he said :

> These boys are good. They are full of fighting spirit and fly with enthusiasm and daring against the best that the Japanese can send against them throughout their long operational tour, which involves some hundreds of hours flying. And in these latitudes even 100 hours is a lot of flying. They have unhesitatingly attacked Japanese Hap floatplanes and shot some down. Even the Spitfire boys respect the Haps, so the performance of the Hudson boys can be assessed at its real value.

In particular the Wing Commander cited as typical the incident of Flying Officer Ray H. Hornby's beating off the attacks of three floatplanes which attempted to shoot up a convoy. After he had caused one of them to smoke, although his ammunition was exhausted, an RAAF Beaufighter came to his aid and they drove off the enemy.

In January 1944 the unit was re-armed with Beaufort aircraft and three months later these were replaced by Mitchells, sixteen of which were on the squadron by May. The Hudson had been a good servant to No 2 Squadron.

No 13 Squadron RAAF was formed at Darwin, Northern Territory, on 1 June 1940. The creation and formation of the squadron absorbed most of the personnel and all the aircraft of two of the three flights of No 12 Squadron.

At this period of its history the squadron's operational duties were, shipping patrols, security patrols and searches. Initially equipped mainly with Avro Ansons, it shortly converted to Hudsons which it flew until 1943. Night flying in Hudson aircraft commenced at Darwin, giving the squadron its first taste of this type of flying. Early in August twelve Hudson aircraft of 8 Squadron landed at Darwin, enroute for Singapore. At this time the Station Headquarters moved from Civil to the RAAF aerodrome. The end of the year saw 13 Squadron continuing its role of shipping patrols which lasted until the latter part of 1941.

May 1941 was a significant month for the squadron, as from the middle of the month there began a series of familiarisation flights to the Netherlands East Indies. The following months the Hudson aircraft were modified by the fitment of Boulton Paul gun turrets.

Towards the end of November there was some anxiety in Australia as the cruiser HMAS *Sydney* was overdue at Fremantle and nothing had been heard from her. Accordingly on the 24th patrols were instituted covering the eastern Indian Ocean where the cruiser had been searching for possible German armed merchant raiders. Hudsons from No 14 and 25 Squadrons at Carnarvon as well as three others from No 13 Squadron were among those briefed. The next day a Hudson from No 14 Squadron sighted three lifeboats, reported their position and directed the rescue of the seamen aboard. These turned out to be Germans from the raider *Kormoran*. They revealed one of the most macabre sea stories of World War II. *Sydney* had approached close to the raider when it did not reply to her challenge. When the cruiser was within range *Kormoran* opened fire and immediately put the warship's for'ard turrets out of action. The cruiser at once replied setting the raider afire amidships. An hour later the German captain ordered his crew to abandon ship. At this time the *Sydney* was on the horizon also blazing amidships and astern. Later, some of the Germans claim to have heard a dull explosion; at all events there were no survivors.

Later again more Germans were seen from the air and rescued, but on the 29th all hope was abandoned for the Australian seamen.

The refuelling of the searching Hudsons was good practice for the ground staff who worked throughout the twenty-four hours, day after day, while the search was on, often having to resort to hand pumps.

Following the search, with the outbreak of war with Japan imminent, orders were received for 'A' and 'C' Flights to move to Laha in Ambon, Netherlands East Indies. At this time the squadron strength was twelve Hudsons of which half were operative from Laha with eight crews. On 16 December advice was received that US aircraft moving from Manilla to Australia would be using the airfield enroute. Subsequently US Flying Fortresses and Catalinas utilized Laha enroute to Darwin.

On 30 December three Hudsons from 'B' Flight were recalled from Namlea to reinforce Laha. At the same time Namlea was advised to be prepared for a Japanese flying boat bombing attack and to prepare the airfield and buildings for destruction in the event of evacuation.

During the early hours of 6 January 1942 seven enemy aircraft bombed and strafed the Laha airfield and building area. A number of buildings and workshops belonging to the Dutch were damaged, however, there were no RAAF casualties. Native villages were also bombed and due to the dispersal of the natives a labour problem existed for a number of days. This raid had an adverse effect on morale at Laha, and the knowledge that no warning facilities were available caused a general evacuation of the camp at night. Trenches were dug into a hill adjacent to the camp area and were used nightly by personnel without the protective covering of mosquito nets and as a result, the incidence of malaria jumped considerably.

At Laha, four days later, a Hudson made two attacks on a four-engined Japanese flying boat, pursuing it out over the Malacca Sea. The enemy aircraft at first attempted to climb away at high speed, but was unsuccessful. It then dived to sea level, but the Hudson proving superior in speed and climb managed to score hits on the enemy. The Hudson was eventually forced to break off the engagement owing to a shortage of fuel.

On 11 January Laha was again raided by the Japanese, 27 bombers escorted by Zero fighters bombed the airfield, dropping approximately 300 bombs and leaving the runway badly holed. The fighters strafed the airfield and succeeded in igniting a fuel dump. Enemy bombings of Laha soon became a daily affair.

At Ambon No 13 Squadron was now experiencing the building up of the Japanese onslaught. It was also having other troubles: malaria was on the increase, and the medical officer was greatly concerned. The incessant raids caused the Laha camp area to be evacuated at night and personnel were billeted in the native villages and a nearby Agricultural College. Hudsons on the ground, US Catalinas off shore and intercepting Brewster Buffalo fighters were all lost.

New Zealand Hudson III of No 1 RNZAF Squadron operating out of Henderson Field Guadalcanal.

New Zealand Hudson III's, notice different roundels on centre aircraft.

Lack of fighter protection against the bombing attacks, and increased enemy action caused the abandonment of the auxiliary base at Babo in Dutch New Guinea. This base was evacuated on 29 January and all personnel were returned to Darwin.

At the same time conditions at Laha had become deplorable and the base became untenable. An umbrella of enemy fighters was over the base almost daily, making operations extremely hazardous. Fighter protection was almost completely lacking, and the approach of a large enemy convoy was reported. For a week to ten days the base had been used only at night with the aircraft dispersing during the day to Koepang, Namlea, and other bases. The maintenance of aircraft was almost entirely neglected, and aircraft had to proceed to Darwin for inspections. The evacuation began when forty-two personnel were returned to Australia by air in Hudsons and Short flying boats. The sick personnel, most of whom were malaria cases were evacuated from Ambon hospital by flying boat. All equipment that could not be salvaged was destroyed. The transmitter motor was made useless and tractors were smashed and dumped from the end of the pier. Rifles were also rendered unserviceable. Prior to the evacuation the Australian troops in occupation were moved from the airfield areas to reinforce the troops defending the township of Ambon. All ground machine-guns, spares and ammunition were handed over to them. Up until the time of evacuation of Laha and Namlea·Nos 2 and 13 Squadrons had lost thirteen Hudson aircraft. Due to the lack of transport from Laha, a number of personnel had to be left behind.

With the Japanese infiltration of the Netherlands East Indies, Koepang Advance Operational Base was next to be evacuated, and during 19 February aircraft of No 13 Squadron assisted in its evacuation.

The same day also saw the first enemy air raid on Australia when at 0955 Japanese dive bombers, escorted by fighters, attacked the RAAF station at Darwin as well as wharves, shipping and the township. Much damage was caused and the Squadron Headquarters, the stores hangar and grounded aircraft were destroyed. Two hours later a further attack developed when 54 heavy bombers carried out a high level pattern bombing of the airfield, seven personnel were killed but No 13 Squadron suffered no casualties.

North-Western Headquarters moved from Darwin to Daly Waters on 28 February and encountered almost chaotic conditions. Maintenance facilities were poor and many of the aircraft were damaged and there was a lack of spares and essential operational equipment as the majority had been destroyed at Darwin. In addition many of the men after experiencing such trying conditions in the islands were in poor physical condition. At times the combined efforts of both No 2 and No 13 Squadrons could muster only two or three operational aircraft between them.

Broome, Darwin and Daly Waters were all attacked during March and two sergeant gunners were killed as their Hudson was damaged whilst landing as a raid took place. The Japanese raids continued into April with the bombers coming over in their usual groups of seven in V-formation. On 2 April seven heavy bombers escorted by three Zero fighters attacked the fuel tanks at Darwin destroying 29,500 gallons of fuel.

In the same month No 13 Squadron began to hit back at the enemy in the Netherlands East Indies and Timor. From this date its programme of reconnaissance and photographic missions, and raids on enemy shipping and ground installations had a small beginning which finally reached a crescendo the following year.

On 13 April during an attack on shipping in Koepang Harbour, a Hudson of No 13 Squadron was intercepted by enemy fighters and the air-gunner was hit by bullets. Although wounded, Sergeant D. Cotsham remained at his gun and succeeded in shooting down one of the enemy aircraft.

On 2 June five Hudsons carried out a strike against the Japanese at Atomboa. The barracks were demolished, fires started, road transport strafed and the area in general machine-gunned. From this time on there was a stepping up in the tempo of hitting the enemy and the attacks reached their peak between mid-August to mid-September when aircraft and personnel of No 13 Squadron were on practically continual operations against the enemy in the Timor area. As a result of these operations the Commanding Officer of the squadron received a letter from the Allied Air Force Headquarters which read:

I wish to take this opportuntiy to commend No 13 Squadron for the excellent manner in which its assignments were performed in the Timor area. The initiative and courage demonstrated during the numerous reconnaissances and photographic missions as well as in the raids made on enemy shipping and ground installations were very gratifying.

I refer particularly to the attacks carried out by nine Hudsons on troops, buildings and motor transports at Mape, Timor on 14 August. All bombs were dropped in the target area and several direct hits were scored. The successful reconnaissance missions which were carried out over Baso Viqueque; Nova Anadia, and Mape Beaco proved to be of the utmost importance. These operations contributed greatly to the successes enjoyed by the Allied Forces during this period and your Squadron can feel justly proud of the part it played.

The letter was signed George C. Kenny, Major-General-Commander.

On 24 December 1942 Nos 2 and 13 Squadrons co-operated in an attack on an enemy destroyer and four transports sighted off Timor. The beginning of 1943 found No 13 Squadron at Hughes, Northern Territory, gradually being rested down after its strenuous operations against the enemy. On 4 April 1943 the last six Hudsons of No 13 Squadron left Hughes for Batchelor and the squadron then became non-operational.

IX

The Kiwi

This is the story of Varley Allen Pedersen, better known as Jim in his native New Zealand. Jim was born on 28 October 1913 at Mananus on the North Island, the only son of a locomotive driver. After school and an engineering apprenticeship Jim took up flying with Waikato Aero Club under the instruction of Harry Lett, a Royal Flying Corps pilot in the First War. Harry says that Jim used to visit him weekly for instruction; he remembers him as a sensitive boy with an inferiority complex. Jim obtained his private pilot's licence in June 1937 and his aim then was to gain a short service commission with the Royal Air Force.

After grappling with mathematics, a subject in which he was not particularly good, Jim qualified for a commission. In August 1938, together with seventeen other short service commission entries, Jim sailed in MV *Rangitata* from Auckland en route for England and the Royal Air Force.

It was with heavy heart that Jim left his fiancée Barbara, his parents and his native country for No 9 E & RFTS at Walgrave in the Midlands. In an early letter home Jim wrote:

England is a hell of a place, one can't see anything for smoke. This location is to leeward of Wolverhampton, Birmingham and Coventry and of course all the smoke blows down on us, making a continuous heavy haze. Seventeen of the boys have been lost to date, and in some cases have finished up seventy miles away. The instructors here really can fly; twice when they have been frisky, nine of them have made a formation and taken the boys up. They fly in arrowhead formation with the wingtip in between the wing and the tail of the next machine, the maximum distance being six feet away from the other aircraft. I have given birth to several sets of twins when a bump throws all the machines in a heap. We are that close that the valve rockers on the next machine can be seen working quite easily. My flying here totalled 42 hours, more than I flew in two years back home.

Further advanced in his training Jim later wrote home from Little Rissington, Gloucester :

The object of being here is to practise our exercises with live ammunition and bombs. We bomb from 6,000 to 10,000 feet and this means releasing the bomb about a mile before reaching the target, as the bomb travels forward at about the same speed as the machine. The time taken to fall 6,000 feet is 24 seconds. As you may guess, this is not too easy and direct hits are not common. For the machine-gunning the pilot flies the machine at about twenty feet above the ground at about 130 mph while the bloke in the gun turret pops away with the Lewis gun. The fighter boys of course use the front guns but as yet we do not.

Yesterday rather a humorous incident occurred. I was up as bomb aimer with a New Zealand lad as pilot. When aiming, one lies flat in the nose of the aircraft and uses a very complicated sight. Owing to the water pouring all over me I was very miserable and did not take much notice of the signals on the ground, which gives orders relating to the bombing. It so happened that a bloody old tramp was making for the target and sheltered from the rain under it. The range officer saw him through his telescope and signalled me to stop bombing. I didn't see the signal and let go a bomb which landed twenty yards from the old bugger whom, I believe, nearly did himself a mischief. He promptly picked up his swag and disappeared in a great haste, and then by coincidence I dropped the worst bomb of the exercise which landed 100 yards from the target. The tramp had just stopped running and thought that he was safe when this bomb burst about ten yards away from him. He didn't stop running then until he reached the marking tower which was a mile away. I received a bit of a stir up for not obeying the signals but I guess that is the best way of keeping people off the range. Lucky for him I was using bombs which do not splinter upon bursting.

Jim passed the examinations for his 'Wings' with an 87 per cent average mark and an assessment of 'Above Average' for flying and was then a fully trained pilot. On 17 August 1939 Jim joined No 220

Squadron of Coastal Command at Thornaby-on-Tees. At this time the squadron was equipped with Avro Ansons but they later re-equipped with Hudsons.

Jim carried out his first operational flight of the war in an Anson on 19 September 1939 and converted to Hudsons the following month but it was not until the following April, on his twenty-second operational flight, that he flew a Hudson seeking out the enemy. In May as already mentioned, Jim flew a Hudson as escort to HMS *Kelly* which had been damaged by a mine and torpedoes and was limping home. The destroyer was under attack by Heinkel He111's but the Hudsons drove them off before they could damage *Kelly* further. On the night of 18/19 May Jim and Pilot Officer Bennett flew together in a Hudson from Bircham Newton to Bremen for a bombing raid on the rail junction. Jim recorded '. . . the whole squadron involved – intense searchlight activity and spasmodic but accurate flak.' The squadron scribe recorded:

Seven of the Hudsons were each given separate objectives and bombed Germany with success, their targets were at or near Wilhelmshaven, Cuxhaven, Hamburg, Bremen and Miersdorf. All aircraft returned safely without their bombs.

On 28 May the whole squadron proceeded by air on attachment to Bircham Newton for operational duties. All available pilots moved with the squadron while at the new base the squadron maintained two standing patrols during daylight hours; one, carried out by single aircraft was a 'crossover' patrol between Ijmuiden and Texel to search for enemy warships or E-boats proceeding down the Channel towards Dunkirk, the other patrol was between North Foreland, Calais and Dunkirk protecting troops on the beach and the ships of all types evacuating the troops across the Channel from Dunkirk. A fuller description of the Dunkirk episode appears elsewhere in the book.

On 1 June Jim's starboard engine was damaged by anti-aircraft fire on a patrol over Texel, the flak was very good and three salvoes were fired before the first shells burst. Two nights later seven aircraft of 220 Squadron carried out a night raid on the oil tanks at Rotterdam. The Hudsons split into two flights and made individual attacks on the target from different directions and different heights and at varying time intervals. It was thought that the result of the attack was successful as large fires were seen burning in the area. The attacks

were made from 8,000 to 2,000 feet but all the aircraft returned
suffering only holes from shrapnel and some broken control cables.
Jim came out through Belgium and reported that he had experienced
extreme difficulty in locating the target. He reported that the flak
above The Hague was very intense and that he was held by a large
number of searchlights.

On 8 June Jim sighted a U-boat but it was able to crash dive
before an attack could be commenced. A week later Jim, again with
Flying Officer Bennett and two crew, together with another Hudson
flew to Malta. The original object was to navigate a squadron of
Hurricane fighters to the Mediterranean island but as the single-
engined fighters had not yet been fitted with long range fuel tanks
the Hudsons took off on their own carrying equipment for the fighter
squadron.

Jim left Thornaby for Tangmere on 17 June and the next day flew
on to Jersey in the Channel Islands of which he wrote :

> This island is a lovely spot, and I was able for the first time to
> enjoy a swim in the sea, followed by a sunbathe on a real snow-
> white beach, and it reminded me of home. We stayed the night
> at a beach front hotel in a little bay. Everything was still and peace-
> ful except for a dull mutter in the air like thunder. This was the
> rumble of guns shelling Cherbourg, a French city only thirty miles
> away. It seemed so strange to be in such a tranquil place while
> the war and all its ferocity were only a few miles distant.

Off again the next day and overflying France the crews saw Brest
blazing furiously and most of north-west France covered in a smoke
pall and the roads packed with refugees. Jim flew across France at
9,000 feet with no opposition, then over Majorca to Algiers of which
he wrote :

> I was in Africa and trying and trying to make myself understood by
> a crowd of officers from the French Air Force, and a considerable
> amount of fun it caused. These fellows entertained us to lunch and
> a mighty queer one it was too; there was plenty of the well known
> red and white wine which is drunk very freely. I chose the white,
> which tasted like sulphuric acid, and the other boys told me the red
> wine tasted like ink. However we had a very enjoyable time for
> about three hours before continuing our flight across North Africa.

I found the country to be quite ragged; we were flying at 8,000 feet all the time and even then we were flying up the valleys with hills and mountains above us on both sides. Below the gullies and gorges appeared amazingly deep and rugged and often had sheer vertical walls. While over this country we ran into a terrific thunderstorm and the air was so rough at one period that I thought our plane, as big as it was, would fall to bits. The sight of the fork lightning zipping just past us did not improve our comfort, and believe me, I do not wish to encounter a North African thunderstorm again. However, we flew through it and went out over the sea again to land at Malta.

The Mediterranean is as blue as people and books say it is. What a change it was from the grey, dull, oily water of the North Sea around England. The heat was about the same as a really hot summer day at home, but as we changed into shorts and topee looking like the real Pukka Sahib, it was very pleasant.

The unfortunate part, however was that we spent only a day there before returning and we were very annoyed by the Italian planes coming over all night and keeping us awake with their bombs. The mosquitos were even more effective than the Italians, so between guns, bombs and mosquitos one didn't get much sleep.

The next day we returned to England, travelling 1,700 miles in under twelve hours. By passenger liner the trip takes twelve days.

On the return trip the Hudsons carried mail, the first to leave the island since the Italians declared war.

Back at Thornaby Jim Pedersen was soon again patrolling over that 'grey, dull, oily water' of the North Sea, dull being the operative word. Toward the end of August Jim attacked some small Danish ships that were flying the swastika. The bombs dropped from his Hudson failed to explode but hits were seen from the machine-gunning. A month later, with visibility down to five miles over a rough sea Jim's crew succeeded in locating a Hudson crew huddled in their dinghy. A few days later his aircraft was fired on by another Hudson as he approached to investigate its markings! In the middle of November Jim's Hudson bombed shipping in Esbjerg harbour and he recorded that Sergeant Smith almost fell out of the window while using the camera. When developed the photographs were not of much use as the squadron report said that bomb explosions were not observed. Jim used his Hudson as a dive bomber, releasing the bombs from 800 feet. The flak was intense but not very accurate. On the same day another Hudson from the squadron shot down an He115 after a mainly front gun attack.

At the end of November Jim piloted one of six Hudsons that set out to attack the aerodrome and seaplane base at Kristiansund. There was thick cloud over the target area and only one aircraft actually hit the target; the others mistakenly bombed other locations and encountered anti-aircraft fire. All returned safely.

From then until the end of the year Jim checked new crews out on Hudsons as well as keeping his hand in carrying out patrols. By the time 1940 ended he had carried out 103 operations. Early in 1941 Jim went to Canada to join Captain Bennett with the Transatlantic Ferry Pool, described elsewhere.

Returning to England in the middle of the year Jim took up instructing duties at No 6 Operational Training Unit at Thornaby. One of his trainees, R. Laughland, writes of this time :

Jim was flight commander and we had a cheerful and happy flight of pilots from all parts of the RAF. Jim used to fly as much as the rest of us, in addition to his duties as a flight commander; he was then a flight lieutenant but promoted to squadron leader in 1942.

We used to pride ourselves that we could fly in any weather. The Anson was such a slow safe aircraft and with our experience of flying all over Yorkshire, following the railway lines we knew every landmark around the airfield and we could be flying when the Hudson flights had 'scrubbed' for the day. So although we were flying obsolete aircraft, under Jim's leadership we thought we were 'all weather' pilots.

Checking through my diaries covering the Thornaby period, I note that I made frequent trips to the local pubs, but never with Jim. I got the impression that he wasn't much of a drinker with the boys.

Ben Fleming says of this time :

Jim would never go on leave so we arranged one for him at a large house in the north of England. We flew him up to be near the place and arranged transport on to the house. He stayed there a week and on return was very happy as he discovered an old car that had not run for years and had fixed it up – a typical gesture, he never stopped working.

While at OTU Jim flew Hudson Mark I, III and V's, a Tiger Moth, Ansons, Oxfords and also piloted a Lysander towing a drogue as a target for gunners. A contemporary wrote of Jim, 'training was not getting at the enemy fast enough'.

While instructing Jim was invited by the BBC in mid-October to take part in the topical programme *In Town Tonight* and was interviewed on aspects of flying the Atlantic. Ever anxious to be back on operations, Jim finally achieved his goal on 22 April 1942, after nine months of passing on the benefit of his experience to new flyers.

Jim was posted to Wick in Scotland to serve with No 48 Squadron on Hudsons. Group Captain E. L. Baudoux was at Wick at this time and writes:

The squadron consisted of approximately 24 Hudsons split into 'A' and 'B' flights. As a General Reconnaissance squadron they were primarily engaged in anti-submarine patrols, convoy patrols, shipping strikes and maritime reconnaissance in the North Sea area. Prime consideration was given to the Norwegian coast and in the main these were night operations, not that there was much darkness at that latitude in the summer. The squadron shared the airfield with No 608 Squadron.

A description of Wick, a little earlier in the year described it as a hell hole, the only aerodrome the writer was ever on where the bar was open twenty-four hours a day; it was needed he said to keep the airmen warm. The snow fell so heavily that they didn't bother to clear it up but just levelled it with a steam roller and marked a soot line down the middle of the runway for the landing aircraft to sight on. At this time a number of Hudsons were lost due to heavy landings which invariably ended with their catching fire.

In the two months prior to Jim's arrival the squadron lost nine Hudsons, including one carrying the commanding officer. The squadron medical officer was aboard another Hudson that failed to return. Coastguards at Dyce reported a Hudson had burst into flames and 'a ball of fire crashed into the sea'. A number of aircrew from the missing Hudsons were later located buried in Norway.

Hudson I flying low over the North Sea . . .

. . . after the runway at Wick had been cleared of snow.

Gordon H. Dunn was an NCO with Jim at the time and he writes:

> In three months we lost twenty crews on operations, just about everyone was a new chum. Jim was my flight commander and in this three months we lost two, if not three, flight commanders. Relating to this is an uncanny happening that I will never forget – the way the beds became empty in my dormitory. It started a couple down from me and continued in a progressive manner. One could predict with almost unfailing accuracy those who would not return.

A week after Jim's arrival Sergeants George Dogue RCAF, Thomas Langoulant and Allen Willis RAAF joined from the Operational Training Unit at Silloth. By this time Jim was 'B' flight commander and joined this crew as a passenger on the first occasion their pilot, Eric Rutherford, took them over the Norwegian coast. He went to show them the ropes and explain the things to watch for; he flew this trip when he was supposed to be on 48 hours leave! The reader will be able to judge the thrill experienced by Allen Willis on his first few operations from a letter he wrote home:

> I am now on operations and stuck away in the north of Scotland, a bleak and desolate dump just near John O'Groats, from where we go out and raid shipping, I thought I had done a bit of flying, but boy! when we go in to attack we get down on the water to about ten feet and go like hell moving from side to side and lifting to put the AA gunners off. The pilot opens up with his front guns to make the Jerries take cover, the bomb doors open, then up and over the masts, at the same time *Wham*, he gets the stick of bombs, then as we scram the gunner in the turret mows the AA gunners down; then the boat sinks and we are all happy. It's a hell of a thrill to get a Jerry lined up in the sights and touch the doings. . .

Jim was busy with his own crew also, on anti-shipping strikes, throughout May during which time the squadron continued to lose Hudsons, usually when tangling in the air with Ju88's.

Gordon Dunn was flying in R-Rodger on 12 May over Aalesund when a shell burst under the starboard wing causing the Hudson to overturn and develop a spin to port. The Hudson fell from 2,000 to

400 feet before the pilot, Flying Officer G. Gates, succeeded in righting it. Gordon wrote:

> Fortunately we were over the harbour and not land at that particular moment. We were preparing to dive down on our way out, dropping bombs at low level on the target ship. However, the unprepared inverted spin saved our lives as it appeared that the ack ack stopped, no doubt thinking we had 'bought it' – mind you, I thought so too. We were then in no position to continue our mission and were thankful to make it home.

Jim took R-Rodger out himself on 16 May for a special reconnaissance in the Skagerrak. The following day R-Rodger flown by Pilot Officer J. R. Paisley, was one of a force of fifty-four aircraft, thirteen of them Hudsons, that flew to south-west Norway to attack German naval units which included *Prinz Eugen*. Eighteen aircraft failed to return, including R-Rodger which was shot down by Leutnant Hartwein of JG5.

There were several reported sightings, and attacks, on U-boats, and in one instance on a basking shark or whale, which in uncertain light and bad weather conditions could have been mistaken for a submarine.

Throughout June Jim Pedersen and his crew carried out anti-shipping strikes and escort duties. On 1 July there was great activity along the Norwegian coast as the ill-fated convoy PQ17 was making its way to Murmansk while the Luftwaffe and U-boats were determined to stop the ships reaching the Russian port. This was the last occasion Jim flew with his regular crew as they were all due for leave; 48 Squadron were keeping watch on the Norwegian coast in case any heavy naval units left harbour to attack the convoy.

Jim was flying on 11 July and three days later the squadron became the first one to be attacked by FW190's. The sighting of these new fighters must have come as a nasty shock to the Hudson squadrons. Although officially still on leave Jim Pedersen teamed up with George Dogue, the Canadian observer, and Australians Thomas Langoulant and Allen Willis; their regular skipper, Eric Rutherford, was away on a residential course for pilots. It will be remembered that Jim accompanied this crew on their first Norwegian sortie. They were not to return from their sixth operation together on 15 July. The official entry records:

Four Hudson aircraft carried out anti-shipping patrols without incident. Another Hudson aircraft was detailed to patrol the Trondheim/Stadlandet area on the Norwegian coast but failed to return from this operation.

Jim's mother received a letter dated eleven days later, which in essence said : 'Your son was captain of a Hudson aircraft which set out for a patrol at 1150/15 from a base in Scotland and has not been seen or heard from again.' The next letter arrived some three years later, part of it read 'in view of the lapse of time and lack of any information concerning them it is deeply regretted that the department is unable to hold out any hope of the survival of the crew, and can only conclude that the aircraft came down in the North Sea and that the crew perished with her.' In the middle of 1946 the Air Ministry wrote with some hard news '. . . a recent report received from the missing research and enquiry service states that the body of your son was washed ashore on 25 July 1942 at the little fishing village of Kya, Norway and will be cared for in perpetuity by the War Graves Commission.'

With the knowledge contained in the letter, and Jim's logbook, Arthur Arculus started the Herculean task of retracing the last flight of Hudson FH378.

After some difficulty Kya was located as a lighthouse, which during the war was manned by the Kriegsmarine. It is possible that the body, recovered at sea, was first taken to the lighthouse before interment. A notice in the German magazine *Jaegerblatt* requesting information elicited a reply suggesting that No 5 fighter wing of the Luftwaffe operating in western Norway and northern Finland was responsible for the destruction of the Hudson.

After five years and three months of worldwide correspondence, following up all trails – some promising and some false, the researcher was finally rewarded when he received a letter from Paul Schalk, a former Luftwaffe *Unteroffizier* :

Yes, I did shoot the Hudson down. We flew with two Me109's and came across Pedersen's aircraft about 80-100 kilometres south of Trondheim near the coast. First the sergeant attacked and received some hits, probably in his radiator. He had to make an emergency landing on the sea and he escaped from the aircraft. I observed him with one eye and Pedersen with the other. He couldn't escape me, the Me109F was too fast. The first burst of fire showed no results, after the second his starboard engine was burning. I had expected that Pedersen would fly to the coast or make an emergency landing on the sea to save the crew. He turned away in the direction of the sea. Suddenly his aircraft soared up and fell from 30-50 kilometres down into the water; his engine was burning so I didn't fire any more at him but could observe the entire crash from close quarters. It's a pity we didn't carry cameras at the time.

I stayed a little while at the site; however I only saw a rubber boat. After my landing at the base I only tanked quickly and set out again immediately to guide the air-sea rescue aircraft which had been alerted. We recovered the sergeant from the Me109 out of the water and could only salvage the rubber boat from the Hudson.

So, at last, the loss of the missing Hudson with two Australians, a Canadian and a New Zealander, was explained.

Had the Hudson returned to base, the action of the crew in shooting down a Me109F would surely have resulted in a medal or medals; as it was these young men from the Dominions and Commonwealth gave their lives for Britain and their story would have remained unknown had it not been for the investigative mind of Arthur Arculus.

'Jim' Pedersen, or 'Pete' as he was better known in the RAF, flew over 1,600 hours, mostly on Hudsons, including 125 operational flights.

X

Channel Dash

In February 1942 the German battleships, *Scharnhorst, Gneisenau* and *Prinz Eugen* were all in the French port of Brest. The first two had been there almost a year and *Prinz Eugen* joined them after the *Bismarck* sortie. In January Hitler had ordered that they return to Germany as firstly they were sustaining damage from Bomber Command attacks, and secondly it appeared unlikely that they would ever be able to break out into the Atlantic unseen.

The Germans conceived a daring plan to bring the ships through the Channel and Hudson aircraft were involved right from the very start of the operation.

The Admiralty realised that the Germans would eventually return the ships to their homeland and obviously the quickest way was up Channel. One of the earlier appreciations of the situation was that the ships would leave Brest during the night, rest up during the day at Cherbourg and continue up through the Straits of Dover in darkness the next night. Later it was thought they would leave Brest during daylight hours, in bad visibility, so as to pass through the narrows in darkness. Both appreciations turned out to be wrong. The Germans planned to leave under cover of darkness and sail their heavily protected squadron through the Straits in daylight.

There had been Hudson patrols from St Eval, in Cornwall, over the area for the best part of a year, covering the night period. The Germans were obviously aware of these patrols but did not know the aircraft were fitted with ASV – a radiolocation device capable of detecting the presence of large surface vessels at ranges of up to thirty miles.

As well as the Hudson patrols there was a submarine stationed at the approaches to Brest, to give an early warning of the battleships leaving.

The three Hudson night patrols were:

(a) the 'Stopper patrol, off the entrance to Brest;
(b) the 'Line S.E.' patrol, between Ushant and the Isle de Brehat;
(c) the 'Habo' patrol, between Havre and Boulogne.

The distance between Brest and the Straits of Dover is about 360 miles. The breakout was fixed for the night of 11/12 February as on that day the Luftwaffe had carried out an extensive meteorological reconnaissance from Bergen to the west of the Faeroes, and from Brest to the west of Ireland, and it was found that a warm front was coming down from Iceland. This front meant low cloud and poor visibility for the Channel area and this decided the date of leaving. In the afternoon a reconnaissance photograph showed the three ships in the main harbour and a bombing attack was laid on for the night. This took place just as the ships were about to leave, and in fact delayed their leaving by an hour. The submarine on watch had left the scene to re-charge her batteries, and if early warning of the German ships leaving was to be known it was all now up to the Hudson patrols.

The 'Stopper' patrol was ordered from 1940 to 0700. The intention was to divide the patrol between three aircraft which would relieve each other in turn. The first aircraft took off at 1827 but on the way to Ushant it encountered a Ju88 and was forced to take evasive action. During the manoeuvre the ASV equipment was switched off and was found unserviceable when it was switched on again. The crew were unable to detect the fault, which was later found to be a blown fuse. The aircraft returned to base, and the crew transferred to another Hudson to resume the patrol at 2238. The third aircraft took over between 2326 and 0310 and the fourth between 0245 and 0701, but nothing was seen. Thus there was a vital gap between 1940 and 2238.

The 'Line SE' patrol was ordered for the period 1940-2340. The detailed Hudson reached its starting point on time but the ASV was found to be unserviceable through an obscure fault. The reliability and efficiency of the ASV instruments at that stage of development and application in Hudsons could not be assessed at higher than fifty per cent. The aircraft remained on patrol until the fault was plainly established but there was no effective reconnaissance over the period. The failure was reported just after 2100 and the aircraft was ordered to return to base and no relief Hudson was sent.

The 'Habo' patrol was undertaken by two aircraft, the first from 0112-0335 and the second from 0435-0631. Nothing untoward was sighted during the course of the patrols.

A comparison of the patrols with the assumed track of the German ships shows that both 'Stopper' and 'Line SE' patrols should have had a good chance of picking up the ships had it not been for the technical failures. The 'Hobo' patrol stood no chance of an intercept as by this time the German ships were still some way to the west.

The German break-out had been well planned and the jamming of British radar on the Channel coast had increased throughout February. The Luftwaffe were to give continuous air cover to the naval force, and minesweepers were to precede the main force which was to be escorted by destroyers.

Through a series of disasters, not until 10.35 am was it known to the British that the German ships were at sea. A Spitfire on patrol reported their presence on returning to base; he did not broadcast the news of the sightings while in the air because he did not wish to break wireless silence.

Some time after midday the gun batteries at Dover opened fire and the motor torpedo boats went to sea. The gun batteries had no successes but the leader of the MTB's sent back an accurate first sighting report which was relayed to the leader of the Swordfish aircraft who was waiting to take off in what was to be a suicide mission. The MTB's withdrew as the inadequately supported Swordfish biplanes made their attack. All six attacking aircraft were shot down. The next scheduled attack was by Beauforts, but these torpedo carriers failed to locate the German force. The following Beaufort force attacked the ships but without result. A mixed force of Beauforts and Hudsons escorted by Spitfires were detailed to attack next. The plan was for the Hudsons to provide diversionary bombing while the Beauforts attacked with torpedoes. It was thought that the Hudsons would attract the early attention and draw off the AA fire.

There was a farce as the aircraft circled Manston, the airfield on the Kent coast between Margate and Ramsgate. The Beauforts formed up on the Hudsons, then the Hudsons came in behind the Beauforts; but they were unable to communicate with each other as they worked on different frequencies. Hudsons H-How, J-Jack, K-King and F-Freddie, unable also to contact the escort, returned to base. The Beauforts set out for the target followed by some of the remaining Hudsons, with Spitfires as top cover. The weather conditions were bad, but Hudson S-Sugar of No 407 Squadron flew in formation with W-William and V-Victor to the battleships, where bombs were dropped from between 900 and 400 feet. W-William did not return. J-Jack of No 407 Squadron flew in formation with P-Peter and a Hudson of 59 Squadron, but the latter returned to its base at North

Mast height attacker of No 407 Squadron RCAF closing up.

Coates without attacking. The remaining two Hudsons flew low over
the ships dropping their bomb load from 1,500 feet P-Peter did not
return.

There were further attacks by aircraft and the Harwich destroyer
force. The large ships arrived back safely in Germany but *Scharnhorst*
and *Gneisenau* were damaged by mines. The Germans lost 17 aircraft
during the operation to 41 lost by the British. It is highly debatable
whether the Germans profited from their successful Channel run as
all three large ships were later put out of action for some considerable
time by air and sea attacks. In Britain however the successful escape
of the German ships through the English Channel caused dismay – the
newspapers demanded an enquiry and the Prime Minister set up a
tribunal to look into the circumstances of the German breakout.

That the Germans used the English Channel, and in broad daylight,
should not have occasioned the Admiralty so much surprise. Ten
months earlier the successful secret raider *Thor*, three times victorious
over British armed merchant cruisers, successfully negotiated the same
route back to Germany. A month later, in May 1941, Captain Grau

conned the large replenishment ship *Nordmark*, which we met earlier, through the Straits in daylight when she returned to Germany after replenishing the *Admiral Scheer*, secret raiders and submarines in the South Atlantic.

I have not seen it mentioned elsewhere but I believe the triumphant passages of *Thor* and *Nordmark* probably suggested to the Kriegsmarine that there was a chance of success when these two ships returned unscathed. Though *Nordmark* did not pass through the Straits undetected, as the Dover War diary for Monday 19 May 1941 read:

There was a moderate south west wind, visibility was moderate improving to good in the afternoon. At about 1030 a radar plot was obtained of a vessel off Gris Nez on a north-east course making a speed of seventeen knots. No further information could be obtained, however, and consequently it could not be judged whether it was an important ship . . . later in the day, between 1730 and 1830 when the visibility improved, a large ship was observed making about fifteen knots eastbound. She appeared to be a tanker, loaded, of about six thousand tons and was proceeding eastward closely escorted by several R-boats and aircraft. The weather was too clear for the motor torpedo boats to be sent out and it was not possible at the time to organise an air attack, but the RAF intended to search the vessel out at dawn and attack. Unfortunately when daylight came the aircraft were fogbound and so another valuable ship escaped unattacked.

With hindsight it is all too easy to see that the Germans, with their vast air cover over ships that could outgun anything the Royal Navy could put out from southern England, only had to fear mines.

It might have been a very different story if the ASV radar on the patrolling Hudsons had been more reliable on that February night.

XI

United States Hudsons attack

Although neutral at the time, the US Navy initiated action at the end of September 1941 to requisition twenty Hudsons that were in production for the RAF. These were delivered the next month and were operational from Argentia in Newfoundland, a base the US Navy had taken over.

Germany declared war on America in the December and in the first two months their U-boats had rich pickings right down the US eastern seaboard, attacking ships that were still lit at night and were chattering on their radios. In the first half of March 1942, just four months after their war declaration, the German U-boats found out to their cost that they could not take the Hudsons of No 82 Squadron of the US Navy too lightly.

At thirty-seven Kapitänleutnant Ernst Kröning was old for a U-boat captain. Before joining the submarine arm he served with the Second Minesweeping Flotilla, transferring in April 1941. He underwent initial U-boat training then joined the 24th Flotilla, for two months, in June. During this time his future charge, *U-656*, was being constructed at the Howaldt Werke in Hamburg. Commissioned on 17 September, the U-boat worked up and stayed with the 5th Flotilla until the end of the year when it joined the 1st Flotilla at Brest. On 4 February it left France for the American coastline and sent its last message back to base at 1743 on 24 February.

Aircraft P-8 took off from Argentia at 1100 on 1 March to conduct an anti-submarine patrol off the coast. The aircraft was returning from its mission at 1330 when suddenly a U-boat was sighted some fifteen miles ahead. The Type VIIC boat was within sight of Newfoundland, and this was the last land any of her crew would ever see.

The Hudson was flying at 600 feet, just below the cloud ceiling; there was a fifteen knot north-west wind at the time. The pilot immediately opened the bomb bay doors, the co-pilot set the fuses to explode at fifty feet. As he came in for his bombing run the pilot noticed that the submarine's superstructure was painted light grey and

122

was cruising slowly on the surface totally unaware of what was to come. It was only just as the Hudson commenced its attack that the U-boat began to crash dive, but at the time the bombs were released all the submarine except the bow was still visible. Two depth bombs were released from between 40 and 50 feet and both landed short on the starboard bow. The point of impact, on the water just short of and alongside the bow, was such as to allow the underwater trajectory of the bomb, thus ensuring the perfect straddle abreast the conning tower at the time of detonation. The explosions were observed by the pilot and crew to be on either side of the submarine as the plane continued on course before making a climbing left turn for better observation. Four or five minutes after the attack oil started to rise and was still rising when the Hudson had to return to base an hour later. On arrival at Argentia the crew were hurriedly debriefed, the Hudson refuelled and rearmed and took off again in company with two other Hudsons to revisit the scene of action.

On arrival oil was seen to be still rising and the plume was moving very slowly cross wind. From this it was assumed that possibly the U-boat may have recovered from the initial attack and was continuing on her original easterly course. The rate of advance was determined by the dropping of smoke lights at the end of the oil plume. The other two Hudsons dropped depth bombs about 600 feet ahead of the oil slick and as a result the oil stopped rising for about a minute, then there were large air bubbles followed by the rise of more oil. The track now showed that the rate of advance was retarded. Two more bombs were dropped, one from the original P-8, before the Hudsons returned to base at dusk.

Two US destroyers were sent to the scene in case there was any possibility that the submarine would be able to creep away during the night and aircraft were despatched at first light covering a radius of 235 miles coming inward to see if there was any sign of the U-boat. They all ceased searching when oil was seen emanating from a source just four miles away from the original source of the previous day. During this day and the next the destroyers dropped thirty-three depth charges with differing depth settings. On 5 March the oil flow increased and samples of it were taken to the Boston Navy Yard for analysis. The oil slick marked the last resting place for Ernst Kröning and his crew.

Just two weeks after the first attack another pilot was rather lucky to sight *U-503*, and his reactions were to prove equally as good

U.S. A-29.

The last variation, the AT-18A. This aircraft without a turret was built as a navigational training aircraft for the USAAF. It will be remembered that this is what the British Commission had in mind when ordering the Hudson in 1938.

A-28A used as a USAAF troop transport.

U.S. Navy A-29.

as those of his colleague. P-9 had taken off from Argentia just before noon on 15 March for a convoy protection patrol. The Hudson was to provide air cover for convoy ON-72. Two hours after take-off the Hudson arrived at the estimated position of the convoy but was unable to see any ships. The pilot commenced a search four miles south of the convoy track and ten minutes later saw a black painted submarine with decks awash less than a mile ahead on the port bow, on a parallel course travelling at slow speed. Probably the U-boat was tracking the convoy the Hudson was seeking. At the time there was a rough sea, a 20 knot wind, light fog and broken clouds at 1,500 feet hiding a blue sky.

The plane was flying at 800 feet at the time and as the pilot came into the attack he opened the bomb bay doors and checked that the bombs were armed. The four bombs were fitted with shallow depth settings set to explode at fifty feet. The pilot could see two periscopes and the bridge on the conning tower, but no crew members were visible. The Hudson was within a quarter-of-a-mile before the U-boat crash-dived. The pilot attacked from the starboard quarter at a line of attack of about 15 degrees. The Hudson was travelling at 185 knots in a slight dive and the bombs were dropped from fifty feet. At the time the stern of the submarine was still visible but had disappeared just prior to the first bomb exploding.

The bombs were carried in the bomb bay, two forward and two aft, set to drop, when released, in a stick spaced at intervals of 0.2 of a second by means of the electric bomb release distributor. For an 0.2 second interval the bomb spacing should have been approximately 60 feet at 180 knots.

Only three bomb detonations were seen and one of the crew stated he saw the stern of the U-boat rise to the surface with the bomb bursts. On return to base it was found that one of the bombs had been released in the 'safe' position. The second bomb dropped ricocheted ahead to the right probably due to a momentary right skid assumed by the aircraft. The bombs were all released short of the target to allow for the underwater trajectory.

Straight after the attack the pilot started a climbing right-hand turn and the co-pilot was able to observe the detonations. He said that immediately after the explosions a large bubble of oil and air about a yard in diameter was seen to rise. This was followed by a large amount of debris consisting of numerous irregularly shaped slabs of cork, some as large as half-a-yard in diameter; a number of smaller

AT-18 USAAF.

pieces of cork, apparently unpainted; about a dozen splinters of wood some a yard long, painted black : and a large oil slick which spread in size to 50 by 200 feet. The oil started spreading down wind immediately and broke up in the sea. The whole action had taken only 25 seconds from the time of sighting to the time of release and says much for the training of the Hudson's crew.

The aircraft was forced to leave the scene after half-an-hour as its fuel was running low. Two further Hudsons were despatched to the scene but were unable to reach the area before nightfall and returned to Argentia.

There had been no need for the further two Hudsons as *U-503*, a Type IXC U-boat, under the command of Korvettenkapitän Otto Gericke, had been well and truly sunk by Hudson P-9.

The U-boat did not have time to signal that it was being attacked. Before joining the U-boat service, the 33-year-old commander had served in the destroyer *Diether von Roeder* from August 1938 until May 1940. After training and serving aboard *U-17* he was appointed to command *U-503* on its commissioning at Hamburg in July 1941. The 2nd Flotilla boat left Bergen on its final voyage on the last day of February 1942 and sent its last signal back to base at 0100 ten days later. The crew aboard the submarine and U-boat headquarters did not know it was US Navy No 82 Squadron that had achieved the sinking, for at the end of the war an inspection of U-boat's operational records showed that its loss was attributed to a 'probable collision with an iceberg'.

Not to be outdone by the Navy Hudsons, a US Army Hudson sank *U-701* off the Atlantic coast four months later.

XII

The Thousand Bomber Plan

In mid-February 1942 a bombing directive from the Air Staff to Bomber Command made reference to 'Gee' – the radar aid to navigation and target identification. The directive said: 'You are authorised to employ your effort without restriction in accordance with the following directions. Clearly this does not warrant pressing your attacks if weather conditions are unfavourable or if your aircraft are likely to be exposed to extreme hazards'. The directive continued:

> In the opinion of the Air Staff, the introduction of Gee will confer upon your forces the ability to concentrate their effort to an extent which has not hitherto been possible under the operational conditions with which you are faced. It is accordingly considered that the introduction of this equipment on operations should be regarded as a revolutionary advance in bombing technique which, during the period of its effective life as a target-finding device, will enable results to be obtained of a much more effective nature.
>
> The period in which this device can be used as an aid to target location and blind bombing will be governed by the ability of the enemy to develop counter-measures when the secret of its nature and operations has been disclosed. Much will depend on the security measures observed in its employment and the care taken by air crews to ensure the destruction of the apparatus and to avoid mentioning or discussing it in the event of their aircraft being forced down over enemy territory. It is unlikely, however, that under the best possible conditions this period will exceed six months from the date of its introduction. It is accordingly of first importance to exploit the advantages it confers to the full. The maximum effort possible having due regard to weather and other hazards should be exerted throughout the period it is thus available, and particularly in the first few weeks of your operations.

The directive went on to say that it had been decided that the primary objective of the operations should now be focused on the

morale of the enemy civil population, and in particular, of the
industrial workers. A list was enclosed of selected target areas within
the scope of Gee. These included Cologne, Essen and Bremen among
others, and all were within the 350-mile range from the bombers'
bases. Cologne and Essen were mentioned for 'transportation and
general industries' and Bremen for naval dockyards. It was suggested
that Essen was the most important of the selected primary targets and
that by attacking it first the maximum element of surprise would be
achieved.

The directive continued :

During the estimated effective life of Gee as a target-finding and
blind bombing device, it will not be possible to equip more than a
relatively small proportion of your force. It is, therefore, of the first
importance that tactical methods to assist the remainder of the
force to achieve concentration, both when the target is capable of
being illuminated and under blind bombing conditions, should be
studied, developed and applied to the maximum possible extent.

The directive concluded :

Finally, I am to say that, although every effort will be made to
confine your operations to your primary offensive, you should recognise that it will on occasions be necessary to call upon you for
diversionary attacks on objectives, the destruction of which is of
immediate importance in the light of the current strategical situation. In particular, important naval units and the submarine building yards and bases may have to be attacked periodically, especially
when this can be done without missing good opportunities of bombing your primary targets.

By May 1942 Air Marshal Arthur Harris, the Air Commodore who
had ordered the Hudsons from America in 1938, was the Commander-
in-Chief of Bomber Command. Early in the month he confided to his
second-in-command that it was his wish to put a thousand bombers
over Germany on the same night. His deputy did a quick count up and
thought that with all Bomber Command, the training groups and
assistance from Coastal Command this would be possible. The Commander-in-Chief of Coastal Command was asked for the use of 250
aircraft, for this was roughly the number that Bomber had lost to

Coastal over the previous year. Sir Philip Joubert replied on the 21st of the month that he thought he could provide the aircraft, consisting of Wellingtons, Whitleys, Hampdens, Beauforts and Hudsons. He suggested that their own East Coast aerodromes were used and that he proposed to use anti-submarine bombs to get the maximum blast effect. The offer was accepted with alacrity. However, the Admiralty intervened and no Coastal Command aircraft were allowed to take part in this first historic Thousand Bomber Raid.

Hitherto the bombers' navigation had not been precise enough to enable the bombers to be 'streamed'; the advent of Gee had changed all that. The concentration-in-time of bombing attacks promised a further advantage, for it would reduce the effectiveness of the German anti-aircraft guns : the target's defences would be saturated. The new tactics were to be tried out on the big raid with the attacking aircraft all taking the same route, thus the period of attack was cut from about seven hours to two and a half – an average of seven aircraft bombing each minute.

It had been decided at the end of May to deliver an attack of exceptional weight on an important German industrial city. On the 30th of the month, full moon, good conditions at home bases and the fact that the necessary forces were standing by, made it important to carry out this attack with the least possible delay, although thundery cloud was known to cover much of Germany. Conditions at Cologne were more promising than at any other target suitable for such an operation, and later weather forecasts showed there was even a chance of very good conditions in the area.

These forecasts were completely confirmed by events. Though very dirty weather was experienced over the North Sea, in which crews of No 4 Group in particular met bad icing conditions, the cloud broke over Holland and at the target could be identified without undue difficulty by every crew.

The mass raid on Cologne, the administrative centre of the Rhine-land, was the greatest Allied air operation ever planned and un-doubtedly achieved the greatest single success in aerial warfare, up to this time. Coming at the end of a month of persistently unfavourable weather it served to emphasise the influence of meteorological condi-tions on the bombing effort. While known weather conditions fre-quently interfered with the use of home bases, they also greatly restricted the selection of targets for any given night.

The organisation of such a vast force astonished many people besides the Germans; it was twice as great as anything the Luftwaffe had even sent over Britain at this time. No 3 Group alone despatched some 250 aircraft, a number usually regarded as a strong bomber force in itself. Operational Training Units of the Command put up 302 aircraft in addition to 64 attached to Nos 1 and 3 Groups. Apart from four aircraft of Flying Training Command the whole force which attacked Cologne was provided by Bomber Command. A further fifty sorties, Bostons of No 2 Group with 16 aircraft of Army Co-operation Command, set out to patrol enemy night fighter bases near the target or along the bomber routes with a view to restructuring the activities of the defence. Fighter Command assisted in these Intruder operations, which were considered by the attacking crew to have been extremely helpful. Some 1,455 tons of bombs were dropped on the area of the city, nearly two-thirds of this total weight being provided by an immense number of incendiaries. In fact, in one night the RAF dropped on Cologne a weight of bombs greater than the Germans released on London in a whole month at the height of the 1940 Blitz.

Early next day the pilot of a Mosquito, the first operational sortie made by this versatile aircraft, observed numerous fires still burning in the central city and in adjoining industrial and residential areas each side of the Rhine. Smoke covered the city and rose to a height of 15,000 feet, making photographic reconnaissance quite impossible. Eventually, when the smoke cleared away, six hundred acres of complete destruction were revealed, and half of this area was situated in the inner city. Nothing on such a scale had hitherto been achieved by any air force. The *Kölnische Zeitung* reported: 'All the inhabitants when they saw the smoking ruins of their city, realised they had seen the old Cologne they knew for the last time.'

The effect on the workers and their families must have been overwhelming. In March and April, Hitler and his spokesmen had tried to persuade the German people that the RAF could only destroy 'undefended mediaeval towns'. The realisation that the most heavily defended cities in the Reich could be treated in an equally terrible manner must have had a tremendous effect on morale throughout Germany.

A total of 1,046 bombers took part in the raid for a loss of 39 aircraft – a loss ratio of some four per cent.

Before the forces assembled for the mass raid on Cologne returned to their normal occupations a similarly organised attack was directed against Essen, in which all aircraft took the same route and the

attack was concentrated into a small period of time. While the
meteorological forecast was not so favourable as could have been
wished, no other high priority target promised better conditions.

Most of the Ruhr towns had suffered considerably in the course of
many RAF raids but the natural smoke screen of this teeming
industrial valley had saved Essen from the full weight of attacks.
Krupps works had been hit and the town damaged from time to time,
but neither had sustained serious damage.

Steps were taken to combat the well-known difficulties which crews
experienced in searching the murky Ruhr in a storm of flak and searchlights. Large scale intruder activity against fighter airfields was again
a feature of the operation. The attack was opened by a specially
selected force of eighteen aircraft which, using Gee, released long sticks
of flares. A strong incendiary force of heavies searched for the target
in the area illuminated and the remainder bombed the resulting fires.

Unfortunately, the weather was not as good as had been expected.
In addition to haze and high broken cloud, a second cloud layer at
3,000-5,000 feet was reported by many aircraft. Under such conditions, as past experience had shown, a definite identification of Krupps
works was most improbable. Most of the flares were released sufficiently
accurately to show the position of Essen. But the halo of light round
the flares due to scattering by the haze prevented most crews from
definitely identifying the town. The majority of the incendiary force
using Gee released their bombs on dimly discerned industrial areas.
The result of these very determined attempts was a scattering of relatively small fires both in and some miles around the town of Essen.
Consequently, the greater part of the main force found only the glow
of numerous scattered fires below the cloud and haze, some of which
were decoys in the surrounding districts. Thus few crews identified
Essen itself and most bombed neighbouring districts which could be
recognised as industrial areas. In Oberhausen, Mulheim, Hamborn
and Duisburg, however, really effective damage was done and large
fires started.

Daylight reconnaissance showed that Essen escaped relatively
lightly, with damage to the railways near Krupps works and to residential property, especially in the south and south-east parts of the
town: Essen had once more narrowly avoided being written off.
Given a few big cloudbreaks in the early stages and the second
Thousand raid might have been as great a success as the first. Nevertheless, the zinc rolling mills, a large boiler works, a tar works, an iron

foundry and several other large factories were hit in Oberhausen. Factories were also damaged at Mulheim and Urdingen, while at Duisburg railway sheds were hit at three points and in the main marshalling yards the locomotive repair shops suffered heavily. Damage was done at other scattered points throughout the Ruhr and, though some craters were seen in open ground between built-up areas and near decoys, most of our bombers successfully aimed at useful targets.

Of the 800 or so aircraft which reached and bombed Essen or other Ruhr towns, 31 were missing, which represented 3.2 per cent, a proportion smaller than usual for well-defended Ruhr targets.

Coastal Command aircraft were allowed to take their place in Operation Millenium II, the raid that took place on Bremen on 25/26 June. While the main stream of bombers attacked the selected target, other commands were in action against enemy airfields or making diversionary raids to draw off the German night fighters.

Thirty-five Hudsons took part in the raid. Their particular target was the Deschimag U-boat building yard, although the overall object of the raid was to completely destroy the North German port. The Hudsons came from Nos 59, 206 and 224 Squadrons. They assembled at North Coates and its satellite airfield at Donna Nook. A dozen Hudsons of No 206 Squadron flew from Aldergrove to North Coates on the night of 23/24, for as they put it at the time 'co-operation with Bomber Command'. On arrival they were sent on to Donna Nook where they prepared for the bombing raid. The twelve Hudsons, in four formations of three took off in the space of ten minutes from 2300 to take part in the raid. Nine of them arrived safely over the target area but they were unable to identify the U-boat yards due to heavy cloud, so their bombs were dropped in the vicinity of large fires. Some of the crews reported seeing night fighters but none of those that returned were attacked. One Hudson bombed Wilhelmshaven and returned with flak damage; the remaining two, S-Sugar and M-Mike, failed to return.

The aircraft of 59 Squadron took off from North Coates at much the same time as the other Hudsons. Two returned early owing to technical breakdowns. Of the remaining ten, eight reported dropping their bombs in the target area; one pilot later admitted that he probably dropped his bombs on a decoy to the south-east of the city and the last Hudson bombed an anti-aircraft battery at Bremervoorde. Most of the aircraft had landed back by 0500 but one that

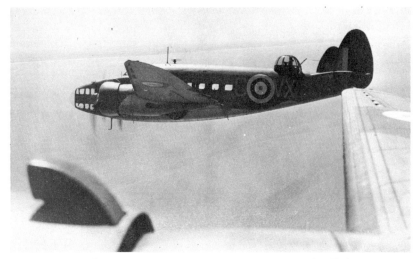

Hudson 1 of 206 Squadron, one of those on the Thousand Bomber Raid.

was forced to land at Catfoss to refuel did not return to base until 0700.

The eleven Hudsons from 224 Squadron had flown down from Scotland for the raid. They took off from North Coates at the same time as the other Hudson squadrons. Hudson A-Able was attacked by two Me110 night-fighters when flying at 8,000 feet; the pilot dived to 6,000 feet and successfully avoided the cannon fire. Later the pilot saw another enemy fighter over Borkum and dived to 4,000 feet where he met accurate light flak. Eventually the Hudson reached Bremen, identified the target and bombed through cloud on to a red glow.

Hudson H-How spent five minutes over the target either side of 0200 and the bomb-aimer dropped the bombs short of a red glow. On the return trip the Hudson was picked up by a searchlight and although a Me110 was observed the Hudson was not attacked.

Hudson K-King was over the target for fourteen minutes before dropping its bomb load and was hit by flak. On its return to base a fragment of heavy anti-aircraft shell was found in the nose of the aircraft although there were no casualties.

Hudson D-Dog bombed the target. On the way back the crew saw an aircraft shot down in the Bremerhaven area. They were fired on by four flak ships while off the Friesian Islands. At the time the

In January 1941 the King and Queen inspected aircraft and quarters of No 206 Squadron and presented decorations at a ceremonial parade. Here the Queen, followed by Princess Elizabeth, alights from a Hudson.

HRH Duke of Kent leaves Hatson in the Orkneys in May 1941 aboard a Hudson 1. The only runway there at the beginning of the war was the main Kirkwall-Stromness road which meant it had to be closed to traffic when aircraft were being operated. HRH Duke of Kent lost his life a year later when the Sunderland in which he was a passenger crashed.

aircraft was flying at only 900 feet and the heavy and light flak proved inaccurate.

Hudson W-William had the daunting experience of seeing three aircraft shot down on the way to the target. While over Bremen some fifteen other bombers were seen and the pilot reported that the flak was in barrage formation, he dropped his bombs on the glow through the clouds.

Hudson L-Lucy encountered some trouble at 0112 when flying at 12,000 feet. The port engine began dropping revs and the oil temperature was seen to be very low. Although the pilot tried to keep his height both defects persisted. Suddenly the town of Wesermunde was seen through a break in the clouds and the aircraft's bombs were dropped from 10,000 feet. The bombs were seen to burst in the centre of the town. The aircraft arrived safely back at base about half-hour before the main force.

Hudson U-Uncle had just released its bombs over the target when there was suddenly a heavy ack-ack burst just below the port side of the aircraft. The blast blew one of the side guns out of the aircraft, and the gun on the other side was blown into the aircraft.

Hudson X-Ray bombed the target just after 0200 and the bombs were seen to burst among warehouses causing fires to break out. The pilot reported the flak was very accurate for height, but not for direction. The pilot arrived back after landing at Thornaby.

Hudson V-Victor plotted its position by observing flak from the towns of Cuxhaven and Wilhelmshaven. The bombs were dropped on Bremen from 10,000 feet through cloud on to the red fires below. The pilot reported encountering heavy ack-ack fire when leaving the area, he says he also clearly saw the decoy fires. Hudson's M-Mike and S-Sugar completed the No 224 Squadron coverage.

After the raid, which had been concentrated into seventy-five minutes, the Hudsons all returned to their parent stations. Two Hudsons were among the 52 aircraft that were lost that night – at this time it was the heaviest loss suffered so far of any night of the war. However the damage to Bremen was great.

This was the last big raid by Hudsons from these squadrons, for all shortly afterwards converted to other aircraft, but Bomber Command continued on with its task and by mid-1943 there were very few targets of any importance that had not been visited by their aircraft.

XIII

Canadian and Dutch Mast-height Attackers

By the spring of 1942 the Canadians of No 407 Squadron RCAF were straining at the leash to get into action. In February they were non-operational with their Hudsons at Thorney Island, practising and training. The favourite target was a sunken ship just off Selsey which had settled on the bottom with its upperworks and masts just showing above the water. In March three Hudsons flew to St Eval on detachment to escort the Naval vessels returning from the Commando raid on the lock gates at St Nazaire. Fully operational at the end of the month they moved to Bircham Newton to be in position when the expected big spring attacks developed. April was spent with the preliminary skirmishes and May saw the attacks develop with a panache and skill rarely excelled. One of the squadron crew members recalls:

We had spent weeks re-organizing and training new crews. The lads were beginning to get restive, this was brought to a head when one of the newest arrivals attacked and successfully bombed an enemy merchant vessel of several thousand tons on 30 April. Several more of our aircraft patrolled the same sea lanes on the following night, and two crews attacked merchant vessels of medium size. To add coals to the fire, one of the successful crews had been with the squadron only a few days.

By this time great interest was shown in the daily aircrew availability roster. Insistent demands for action from all crews made it difficult for the despatching officer to distribute the flights. Several crews were accused of hogging all the fun.

On the evening of 3 May two Hudsons led by the Wing Commander took off in the darkness on a reconnaissance of the waters off the Dutch coast. There was moonlight over the sea but the leader was able to make out other lights on the water. The second aircraft went straight into the attack while the leader made a circuit as the flak came skywards. The leader swung his Hudson away from the scene to call up base and ask for reinforcements before committing himself to the attack. He had seen twelve ships of medium tonnage silhouetted against the silvery sea.

The first attacker had fully alerted the ship's gunners and they were ready for the attack, they even started firing while the Hudson was out of range. The Wing Commander selected the leading and largest vessel as his target as he flew from up moon to attack. He came in over the rim of several other ships, which were all pumping shells skywards, suddenly dipped the nose of the aircraft and dive-bombed the ship, releasing his bombs from four hundred feet. A moment after pulling away from the scene the aircraft gave a violent shudder and a crew member who had been standing in the astro hatch crashed to the floor. At the same time a brilliant flash was seen from the bombed ship. The pilot now really came right down on the crest of the waves and made good his escape away from the flak.

Back at base the Wing Commander found that the other Hudson had returned minus part of his aerials and an escape hatch; unfortunately the pilot could not confirm any hits.

Three other Hudsons had taken off within fifteen minutes of base receiving the position of the convoy, but they were not having things their own way. One failed to locate the convoy at all but the others were finding an intense barrage of light and heavy flak awaiting them. When within half mile of the target an explosive shell pierced the nose of one of the Hudsons and continued through the instrument panel, through the pilot's seat finally lodging against the armour plating behind the pilot where luckily it failed to explode. Nevertheless, the pilot was seriously wounded and suffering intense pain. He was, however, able to direct the aircraft through the flak, although it was hit again and a small fire started. The wireless operator put this out, the pilot reached base and made a good landing before being rushed to hospital.

The remaining Hudson now attracted the full fire power of the convoy but the pilot pressed on and attacked the biggest vessel he could see, setting it on fire. He was then hit in the starboard engine which caught fire and stopped. At this time the Hudson was less than a hundred feet from the sea but the pilot regained control, put out the fire before returning to Bircham Newton where he made an excellent landing with one engine.

Four days later a large convoy was again reported off the Dutch coast and within thirty minutes twelve aircraft were off the ground and flying in formation, led by the Wing Commander, they set course for the convoy. The search began when they arrived at last light. One of the pilots related :

With darkness falling, it was necessary to switch on the station keeping lights in order to retain our relative positions, although there was a chance of encountering enemy fighters. We moved up and down the coast, several miles off shore, all eyes peering into the growing darkness ahead. Twelve aircraft, flying in fairly close formation only several feet above the sea, is trying enough at any time. Add to this the fact that we were searching for a heavily armed convoy and keeping a wary eye open for hostile aircraft at the same time, the situation becomes a little strained. Fortunately, these tactics only lasted for about half-an-hour when the first air-craft saw the outline of the convoy, almost directly below us.

Off went the lights and at the same moment, up came the flak. The convoy was sailing in line astern formation. As we went down the line, ship after ship opened up until the whole area was filled with accurate tracer. At almost the same time, the heavier guns opened up and a cross fire endeavoured to box us in. Shells began to explode uncomfortably near us.

Leading the rest of the aircraft down the line of the convoy, approximately a quarter of a mile to our starboard, the Wing Commander turned in towards them as we passed the ninth ship. The remainder of the squadron followed suit, each picking out a ship and roaring in to the attack. If I had thought the previous engagement with a German convoy was a tough assignment, I found I had still much to learn. The majority of the twelve ships of this convoy were about five thousand tons and equally well armoured.

As we went in to attack a ship of about six thousand tons, it seemed impossible that we could get away unscathed. But we did. Turning in below deck level we released the bombs. We had to make a sharp climbing turn to avoid hitting the mast. From several thousand feet, it is possible to see flak coming, and take evasive action. With the muzzles of the guns only twenty feet away, one has to hope for the best. A terrific flash lit up the area we had just left and the gunner reported that half the stern of the ship had been blown into the air. This was confirmed by the crew of an aircraft which was attacking another ship. While this was going on, our gunner had been pouring lead into a flak ship which was acting as escort to the vessel we had attacked. He silenced one or two of its guns. As we bumped away from the scene, the flak appeared to become more accurate and it followed us for half a mile or more. For the next half hour we could see explosions and shells bursting on the horizon.

One of the biggest vessels damaged on the operation was attacked by a Canadian sergeant who was on his first operational flight. He released his bombs from mast height, causing a big explosion on the stern of the vessel. His aircraft was damaged during the attack. But he managed to retain control and he brought his aircraft back safely.

Meanwhile, the remainder of the squadron had also dumped their loads. Seven ships were definitely hit. From this operation, all the Hudsons returned safely to base, although a number were considerably damaged. Fortunately, no one was wounded.

During the following week the squadron had time to mend its wounds and prepare for other sorties. Although a number of operational flights were made nothing was sighted.

On 15 May a convoy was again reported off the Dutch coast and Hudsons from No 407 and the Dutch No 320 Squadron, with whom they shared the base, took off. The Dutchmen were first to arrive and attack, so the enemy were well alert when the first Canadians arrived. The leader, a pilot officer flying Hudson O-Orange, attacked a large vessel that was lying close to a destroyer. He went in at mast height but as he did so he was wounded in the hands, arms and leg, and both engines on the plane were severely damaged. The pilot brought his aircraft back to base but before a landing could be made both engines failed completely, and the Hudson crash-landed on the edge of the airfield. One member of the crew was killed, the other two received a broken collarbone and a fractured spine and the pilot added to his own injuries by breaking an ankle.

Hudson M-Mike attacked a motor vessel that was estimated to be 3,000 to 4,000 tons. After dropping his bombs, the pilot says the aircraft was given a very definite lift as there was a brilliant explosion which reflected in the cockpit of the aircraft. As the aircraft drew away the gunner observed two flashes on another vessel which were presumed to be hits made by the other attacking Hudson, S-Sugar. Unfortunately this aircraft failed to return to base.

The second formation was led by Hudson K-King; the pilot attacked a medium-sized motor vessel from mast height. The gunner saw a tremendous explosion on the stern and the ship was left burning. The observer was wounded in the foot and all instruments and hydraulics on the aircraft were useless but the pilot was able to make a belly-landing at base.

Hudson Q-Queenie attacked a larger ship from mast height hitting the target amidships, at the same time the pilot saw another Hudson making for the same ship having turned away from its original target after observing balloons. This Hudson made a direct hit on the stern of the motor vessel then burst into flames diving into the sea. This was one of the three Hudsons that failed to return.

Hudson V-Victor had returned to base early with engine trouble, Hudson R-Rodger had crash landed at Coningsby and all the crew were killed. Hudson W-William returned damaged after attacking a small motor vessel which was hit with one bomb. The aircraft's port bomb door, starboard flap, port tyre and port motor were damaged, the aircraft was losing oil but it was brought safely back to base. Three Hudsons failed to return.

The following morning a reconnaissance aircraft reported several merchantmen beached off the Dutch coast.

The next few days were particularly trying for the Maintenance Section. Aircrews rested up after their strenuous efforts.

Towards the end of the month, in which twenty-five attacks were made by the squadron, one of the older pilots came across a ship on fire, the result of an earlier attack by another crew. In the light of the fire, he saw another vessel taking this one in tow, and a third nearby whose boats were busy picking up survivors. During this time the gunners on board the vessels had not been idle and sent up a considerable reminder of their presence. Attacking from mast height, the pilot released his bombs, straddling two of the ships and causing almost certain hits. Flashes were seen, but owing to the light from the vessel. the crew were unable to see exactly what had happened. The rear gunner sprayed the ships with lead.

The following night a Hudson pilot attacked a 5,000-ton vessel from below deck level, scored a direct hit with several bombs, then in an attempt to avoid the flak barrage flew his aircraft in just above the water. He was a little late in pulling back the control column when he reached the vessel. A large mast loomed up from nowhere and ripped off a bomb door. Although the pilot evaded most of the flak,

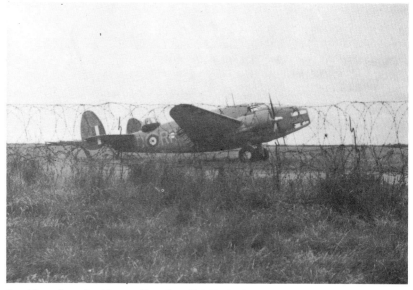

Outsiders view of a No 407 Squadron RCAF Hudson at North Coates.

Dutchmen in their distinctive Naval attire work side-by-side with their **RAF** counterparts on a No 320 Squadron Hudson.

one shell penetrated the bottom of the aircraft and slightly wounded the gunner.

In June there was some anxiety at Bircham Newton as No 407 Squadron had twenty-five complete trained crews and only nine Hudsons, half of which were unserviceable. Aircraft were obtained from squadrons that were transferring from Hudsons.

The Canadians knew it was all worthwhile when in the middle of June there was a report in the Swedish papers saying that Swedish shipping owners were protesting that their ships were being used to transport iron ore to Rotterdam. They said in view of the high casualty rates and continued sinkings they would not in future allow their ships to sail to Holland. Apparently the efforts of the squadron and Coastal Command as a whole had accomplished their purpose to a degree – there had, however, been a high price to pay as the squadron had lost twelve crews on operations in two months.

This attrition could not be allowed to continue and the newly arriving rocket-firing Beaufighters were thought more suitable to attack the heavily defended coastal shipping.

After the St Nazaire escort in March, the shipping attacks in April and May, the Thousand Bomber raid in June, the squadron chronicler was left to record that the only command they had not served in was Army-Cooperation!

In November the squadron transferred to Thorney Island again with their Hudsons and later transferred to Gibraltar where they operated with Vickers Wellingtons.

When Holland was overrun by the Germans in the spring of 1940 several members of the Royal Dutch Naval Air Service were able to escape to Britain in their Fokker seaplanes. All told, only 27 aircraft of the Marine Service survived the disaster. About 250 men, air and ground crew, reached England and initially the crews were formed into two units, No 320 and No 321 with the latter flying Avro Ansons on convoy duties.

In February 1941 the two units were amalgamated to form a new No 320 Squadron. The No 320 Unit had been converting to Hudsons at Leuchars for five months and now the new squadron was posted to the Operational Training Unit at Silloth in Cumberland to complete their training on Hudsons. Here the training was intense and included sighting, gun-stripping, fire-control, link-training, manipulating Bendix turrets and Browning machine-guns, aircraft recognition and range estimation. In addition English lessons were given to all flying crews and other personnel. There was navigational training, gun practice on sea-markers and towed-targets. Also included was dual and solo flying, night and day, regional control practice and finally bombing practice off North Coates.

During 1941, the five squadrons, Nos 48, 53, 59, 500 and 608 converted to Hudsons, and together with No 320 and the Canadian No 407 'Demon' Squadron began training on anti-shipping duties.

After a spell at Leuchars No 320 Squadron moved down to Bircham Newton in Norfolk in the middle of April 1942, transferring from No 18 to No 16 Group and became fully operational from there at the end of the month. The main task of the squadron was to undertake 'Rover' patrols. These patrols were low-level searches for suitable shipping targets by two or three aircraft. These raids were made at mast-head height and both bombing and machine-gunning took place. The enemy soon increased their protection and just a month after becoming operational No 320 Squadron fell foul of one of these heavily defended convoys on 30 May.

Six aircraft led by their squadron leader, flying Hudson NO-F, took off at 2300. Some two hours later they sighted a convoy north of the Friesian Islands. The convoy consisted of seven motor vessels and no less than eight escort vessels. First into the attack was Hudson K-King; the pilot selected for himself a motor vessel of just under a thousand tons. He brought his aircraft down to mast-height and straddled ten bombs across the vessel. There was an explosion on the deck amidships and the vessel burst into flames. The pilot who made his attack from seawards then ran into heavy flak from the shore batteries as well as light flak from the convoy. Later he had to take evasive action to escape from an enemy night-fighter.

The pilot of Hudson R-Rodger was able to observe and attack a motor vessel of about 6,000 tons. The pilot came in at deck level before dropping his ten bombs. The results were spectacular, there were heavy explosions, a brilliant red flash and debris flying in the air. The aircraft received a heavy jolt. The crew estimated that four of the bombs had struck the ship. The pilot reported, that contrary to previous experience, the flak was held by the convoy until two seconds before the bombs were released, then light, heavy and medium flak shot up. Only the Hudson's gun turret was damaged.

When flying at 100 feet the pilot of Hudson P-Peter sighted a motor vessel of some 6,000 to 8,000 tons making a speed of about six to seven knots. The crew kept the vessel in sight as the pilot climbed to

2,500 feet to get in a dive bombing attack. The pilot dived into the moon across the beam of the vessel and released his stick of bombs at 800 feet. As the Hudson pulled out from the dive an explosion was seen on the port side of the ship at the stern. The aircraft encountered very heavy flak from all sides. As course was set for home the crew saw a big fire at the rear of the convoy which they thought was an aircraft burning in the sea.

Hudson L-Love arrived a little after the main force, found the enemy alert and one ship on fire. The pilot made three attempts to attack from the seaward side but each time he approached the convoy a Ju88 night fighter came down moon following the Hudson. The enemy aircraft closed to within 200 yards but no attacks were made. The Hudson pilot jettisoned his bombs after the third unsuccessful attempt on the convoy, turning for home and was followed by the enemy twin-engined aircraft for nearly fifty miles.

Hudson L-Love, like Hudson P-Peter, landed at the satellite airfield of Docking. It turned out to be a costly raid for the squadron as both Hudson N-Nan and F-Fox failed to return; it will be remembered that the squadron leader was piloting the latter aircraft.

The determined Dutchmen continued to harry the enemy, carry out patrol and escort duties throughout the year. In August the squadron were allocated some additional Hudsons and the following month all their aircraft were fitted with ASV.

After this No 48, the Canadian No 407 and No 320 Squadron were the only Hudson squadrons on anti-shipping patrols. In March 1943 No 320 Squadron was taken out-of-line and transferred, less aircraft, to Bomber Command, converting to American Mitchells under the command of No 2 Group.

XIV

Rescued

'One of our aircraft is missing.'

These terse words usually followed the announcement of an attack on enemy-occupied territory. With the Hudson, because of the nature of its duties in Coastal Command necessitating long sorties over the sea, the loss was often totally unaccountable. Statistics were to show that less than fifty per cent of missing Hudsons were actually lost making attacks, the rest disappeared without trace. There can be no doubt that many of them attempted to land on the sea after being damaged in a raid or running out of fuel but very few crews survived to tell the tale.

One of the first successful ditchings was made by Flight Lieutenant D. P. Bamber on 11 March 1941. The pilot was with the Photographic Reconnaissance Unit then based at Heston. He had completed over 2,000 flying hours on all types and some 200 of these were on Hudsons. He with his crew comprising a navigator, air gunner, photographer and wireless operator was detailed to carry out a photographic reconnaissance at the German port of Cuxhaven in broad daylight.

The Hudson crossed the coast just north of Clacton, proceeded over the North Sea and was photographing the port at the mouth of the river Elbe from 8,000 feet when it was suddenly hit by enemy fire. There were three holes in the tailplane and one in the starboard rear wing petrol tank. The fuselage was undamaged and none of the crew were injured. Because of the fuel leakage the pilot thought it would be touch-and-go whether he would be able to reach the English coast and he notified Heston accordingly.

The navigator gave the pilot a course that would bring the Hudson back to England the shortest way. The aircraft was losing height all the time and down below the sea was rough. The wireless operator kept in touch with base continually; the English coast was sighted ahead and the crew thought the faithful Hudson might just make it. The aircraft was now at 800 feet and the pilot could see a trawler some miles ahead, he aimed for this just in case the engines cut before he reached the coast – and it was just as well he did – for suddenly with the fuel gauge reading zero both engines cut. There was a 25-30 mph surface wind blowing. The pilot told the crew he was going to ditch and to hold tight. He released his own harness so he would not be trapped when the Hudson hit the water. By this time the aircraft was within one and a half miles of the coast at Cromer.

The pilot kept the flaps and undercarriage up and hit the water up wind and along the line of the waves at a speed of 90-100 knots. He smashed his head against the instrument panel receiving deep gashes to his forehead and temple. Other members of the crew, except the wireless operator, received minor injuries including cuts and a badly strained knee. At this time of the war there was a shortage of life-jackets and Bamber was not wearing one. All the rest of the crew inflated their Mae Wests before the plane touched down.

Bamber had the aircraft fully under control as it landed. The non-retractable tail wheel was the first part of the aircraft to touch. The nose then flicked down violently and the machine came to an abrupt stop. On coming to rest the water level ran from a point on the fin about nine inches above the tail plane leading edge, to the top of the engine nacelle. About forty seconds later this changed to a more nose-down attitude : the water line from the top of the tail-wheel to the bottom of the pilot's windscreen.

When the Hudson came to rest the crew jettisoned the door, three escaped through it while the pilot and wireless operator escaped through the window almost opposite. The pilot managed to drag the valise-type dinghy through the escape window but when he pulled the life-line nothing happened. There was no sign whatever of inflation; the compressed air bottle had failed to function. Luckily the uninflated valise had some buoyancy in it and three of the crew managed to cling to it. The machine sank nose down in just over a minute after landing.

After the Hudson had disappeared the crew tried unsuccessfully to keep together. The pilot who was without a life-jacket managed to take off all his clothing except his shirt and one shoe. Luckily he was picked up by the trawler just over an hour after his enforced landing. He learned later that the rest of the crew, with the exception of the wireless operator, were rescued at about the same time. The unfortunate wireless operator, the only uninjured member of the crew, was not seen again.

Interviewed later, Bamber was of the opinion that probably many Hudson losses were caused by pilots attempting a flying boat type of alighting – gliding in with the forebody touching first. He thought that the shape of the bottom of the fuselage would then cause the machine to dive straight in, irrespective of whether or not the perspex nose broke. He emphasised that a flaps down landing would almost certainly make the machine dive nose down into the depths. Another possibility he thought would account for the loss of Hudsons on ditching was that a pilot, realising he was going to have to land on the sea, would be most anxious to dispose of his bomb-load, thus lightening the aircraft. However, if the bombs were unloaded from say 1,000 feet as the machine was coming down, there would not be enough time for the bomb doors to close before the aircraft hit the sea. Once again the Hudson would immediately fill with water and sink like a stone.

At this period of the war most Hudsons carried door-type dinghies, although Bamber's aircraft carried the valise type. None of the door-type dinghies had been recovered from several lost Hudsons. Reasons put forward for this included the probability that the functioning of the immersion switch unit was delayed, that some Hudsons operated without them or that the electric plug connection by the door was left unfastened.

Bamber thought that in some cases the crew may have jettisoned the door, with dinghy attached, prematurely. He thought that the buoyancy of the uninflated dinghy would not be sufficient to keep it afloat if it remained attached to the door.

As a result of the interviews with Flight Lieutenant Bamber, revised instructions on ditching were issued to Hudson crews. Tests had confirmed that there was a dangerous tendency to pitch the nose down if the Hudson was landed on water with the flaps down and it was recommended that flaps be kept fully retracted for forced landings on the sea. The pilot and wireless operator were to leave by the pilot's escape hatch and the navigator and rear gunner by the sextant hatch. It was stressed that opening the cabin door and the starboard parachute exit could cause the fuselage to flood more rapidly and that if the door was jettisoned the dinghy could be lost.

Despite all these recommendations the losses of Hudsons and crews landing on the sea remained high. Although their bad ditching properties were well-known, Hudsons were used for air-sea rescue work. The pilots were prepared to take the risk as at any time, whether in war or peace there can be no job more rewarding or satisfying than saving the life of a fellow man. The Hudson was often called upon as a search aircraft and the crew kept their eyes peeled over the ocean for a small dinghy containing airmen who had crashed into the sea. Their concentration was intense and at the end of a search they were inevitably worn out. On the rare occasions they actually sighted a dinghy and a rescue was effected they felt the immense sense of elation that only such a success can bring.

One month after Bamber had ditched, a Whitley was one of a bomber force which set out to raid Berlin on the night of 17 April. The German capital was almost at the maximum range for the Whitley which was then becoming obsolete and being phased out. Unfortunately on the way back from the target navigation was slightly out and the aircraft flew too close to the air defences of Hamburg where it was attacked by enemy night fighters and both engines were hit. The port engine stopped and the pilot found difficulty in maintaining height on the remaining one. While still some ninety miles short of the coast the starboard engine caught fire and the pilot had no alternative but to ditch. The fuselage and starboard mainplane were well ablaze as the aircraft hit the water. The crew of five scrambled out with the dinghy and emergency pack, but in the haste the dinghy was launched upside down and the contents of the emergency pack dropped out – all except two distress signals. The crew managed to get aboard the upturned dinghy and paddled away from the stricken aircraft which exploded when they were only thirty yards away.

It was a very dark night and the sea was extremely rough but the crew were confident they would soon be rescued because the wireless operator was sure his ditching signal had got through. The sea, however, was too rough for the crew to try and right the dinghy and they remained exposed on the smooth underside. On the first day a number of searching aircraft were observed and at last a Whitley spotted them, but lost them again in the very high seas. On the dinghy two men were continually paddling towards the west, a third was baling out with a shoe or empty cartridge case and the others kept an eye out for aircraft. Night came on again, the sea was still high and the crew's spirits dropped a little. They dropped even more the next night after another day in the North Sea when no aircraft at all had been observed. On the third day the sea subsided a little but by now the crew were too weak to risk getting into the water to attempt to right their dinghy. Fortunately, the wind had also dropped and the crew were cheered when a number of aircraft were seen.

On this day the crew of Hudson U-Uncle of No 220 Squadron were ordered to carry out a creeping line ahead search to try to locate the dinghy. At the extreme end of their search line they sighted an object on the surface about one mile distant. It was the Whitley's dinghy with the crew of five in their flying kit and yellow jackets, two of them waving their paddles. Sending a sighting report, the Hudson dived to 200 feet over the dinghy, dropped a container and saw it retrieved within ten minutes.

The aircraft circled the dinghy and flashed a series of messages that a high speed rescue launch was on its way. At dusk flame floats were dropped from the aircraft at half-hour intervals. Shortly afterwards a Hampden arrived and dropped Lindholme Gear which consisted of a new dinghy, four containers of provisions and included warm clothing. Once the crew had climbed into their new rescue dinghy the Hampden disappeared. The Hudson continued to circle and fired off Very lights until its supply was exhausted, it then switched on its navigation lights and these were kept burning until the crew were rescued just after 2300.

We now move on nine months to the Air-Sea Rescue Hudsons of No 279 Squadron. On the morning of 30 January 1942 one of the squadron's Hudsons took off from Bircham Newton with the dual task of carrying out the routine duty buoy inspection and to search for a missing aircraft of No 500 Squadron, or signs of possible survivors in a dinghy.

The patrol proceeded normally for the first two hours, the aircraft flying at 500 feet. About ten miles south of Smith's Knoll a snow shower was suddenly encountered. The pilot switched on the de-icer, carburettor heater and the pitot head heater and no ice was seen forming. As a severe snow-storm developed, the pilot asked the navigator for a course to the coast; they followed this new course but encountered even heavier snow, cutting visibility to nil. They descended to sea level but had to climb again to 500 feet on account of bad icing conditions.

All the flying instruments failed. The ASI fell back to 100 knots; the gyro horizon showed a steep climb, and the pilot pushed the stick forward to avoid stalling. Almost two seconds later, the pilot and navigator saw the sea immediately below; the pilot put his feet on the dashboard and assisted by the navigator, pulled out of a steep dive, but hit the sea hard with the bottom of the aircraft as they jettisoned the escape hatch. They then regained height but again dived to the sea inadvertently and hit it violently losing the navigator's log and maps through the open escape hatch.

Three minutes later they were out of the snow, and continuing on course, thankful to be alive, sighted land and recognised the coast near Lowestoft. The instruments were now working normally although the aircraft was unable to contact base on R/T. They landed just before midday.

Two months later there was another 'bouncing' incident when a Hudson of No 59 Squadron was taking off from North Coates in extreme darkness and haze in the middle of the night; the aircraft hit a dyke. Damage was caused to the pitot head and starboard oleo leg. The wheel was torn off, complete with axle and vertical stub. The pilot was completely unaware of his loss, but realised that his air speed indicator was unserviceable and so informed base of this fact. Base diverted him to Leuchars but visibility there was poor, so prudently the pilot jettisoned his bombs over the sea, flew further north and in better visibility sighted Crail airfield. It was now that the crew noticed that the port wheel was stuck down and the other was missing. The Hudson fired a distress signal and received a reply instructing it to land. Owing to a fire in the hydraulic system the flaps would not lower, and a belly landing was made without their aid. This was skilfully achieved with only slight damage to the bomb-doors, bulk-heads and propellers. None of the crew was injured. The missing leg was later found in a field adjoining North Coates and at a subsequent inquiry the accident was believed to be due to the fact that the airfield was in a soggy condition which unduly lengthened the take-off run.

After these two incidents which demonstrate the capacity of the Hudson to withstand severe damage and still survive, we move on a further five months to August 1942, when two incidents happened in different parts of the seas round Britain which again emphasised the value of the sharp eyes of Hudson crews. Nine rescued airmen had them to thank for saving them from spending the rest of the war in captivity.

On 16 August a motor launch sailed from the Scilly Isles, met up with three other launches and was told to await further orders which arrived just after midnight. All four boats were ordered to search on a line in a given position for three rubber dinghies containing seven airmen. These airmen were the crew of a Wellington and one survivor from a Sunderland.

At first light the launches were joined by three Hudsons and a

Beaufighter, the Hudsons carrying out reconnaissance and the Beaufighter providing air cover. Shortly afterwards three enemy Arado
Ar196 seaplanes were seen about three miles to eastward and these
were driven off by the Beaufighter after they had attempted to attack
the boats. Fifteen minutes later one of the Hudsons circled and
signalled to the boats to change course and proceed at maximum
speed. Ninety minutes later the dinghies were sighted and the seven
survivors were picked up safely.

Two Fw190s appeared and came in and made a determined attack
on the boats. Two of the motor launches opened fire and secured hits
on one aircraft, which thereupon broke off the action, badly damaged
and smoking. The second aircraft also then broke off the action.
Shortly afterwards a Focke-Wulf Kondor and a Ju88 were sighted.
The Kondor kept at long range and made no attempt to attack but
the twin-engined Ju88 made a bombing run and was driven off by the
Beaufighter. The motor launches asked for a stronger fighter escort
and when reinforcements arrived the Kondor prudently disappeared.
Ten hours after they were sighted the rescued airmen were landed
safely at Newlyn Harbour.

Twelve days after the South-Western Approaches rescue two
launches were ordered to sea early one morning by the Flag Officer
Humber to search at daylight for two airmen who had crashed into
the sea twelve hours previously when their Beaufighter suffered engine
trouble.

When the rescue launches were in the estimated position of the
dinghy, three Hudsons flew over and directed them to the east. The
boats continued on course for another half-hour by which time they
were only thirty-three miles off the north coast of Holland. A Do24
flying-boat was sighted flying east. The boats altered course and ten
minutes later the flying-boat was again sighted, this time flying south.
Shortly afterwards a Hudson approached at a height of only fifty
feet, circled, and made off on a north-westerly course. The boats
turned to follow the Hudson and after thirty-five minutes the dinghy
was sighted and the airmen picked up. The Hudsons then left and
five minutes later a Do17Z circled the launches and was later joined
by two similar aircraft and a Ju88. The guns on the launches were
manned and trained on the circling enemy aircraft who frequently
dived to not more than fifty feet, but no aggressive incident occurred
and after an hour the enemy aircraft flew off. An hour later still
the boats were ordered to alter course to search for another dinghy.

After a fruitless search that took six hours the visibility was deteriorating and the boats returned to land the survivors at Immingham.

The rescued airmen said that they were first sighted by a Ju88 which then called up the Do24 flying boat. This was chased off by the Hudsons shortly before the rescue. It appears probable in this case that but for the timely arrival of the Hudsons the enemy flying-boat may well have landed on the sea and taken the airman prisoner. The rescued squadron leader and his sergeant observer had every reason to thank the Hudson crews.

The rescue of the crew and passengers of SS *Buchanan* three months later, in November 1942, was headlined in the popular press as 'The greatest rescue of the war'. In fact the rescue was described as the RAF's greatest rescue, but this was misleading for it was a combined effort by the Royal Air Force, the Royal Navy and the merchant service. As expected, Hudsons played their full part in the rescue.

SS *Buchanan* was torpedoed approximately 500 miles west of Ireland by *U-224* on the evening of 12 November. The 73 passengers and crew took to their four lifeboats, which were in charge of the captain, first, second and third officers.

One lifeboat was sighted by an aircraft of 201 Squadron on the morning of 16 November, by which time the survivors had already spent four wet winter nights in the cold Atlantic. The pilot was able to see there were twelve people aboard the lifeboat. Later in the day, unbeknown to the RAF the crew of this lifeboat were picked up by another merchant vessel that was sailing independently. This was the second officer's boat, the rescuing ship had maintained wireless silence, and so it was not known for three days that the dozen survivors had been rescued.

Meanwhile HMS *Sardonyx*, which had been searching for a raft, was diverted to the lifeboat search on the 18th but, being already short of fuel, was forced to return to base the next day. On the way back she sighted rockets in the evening, and as a result of this a Hudson of No 220 Squadron took off from Northern Ireland to square-search the area. A Sunderland of No 423 Squadron was also in the area and it was this aircraft which sighted a lifeboat that proved to be the first officer's boat, in the morning of the next day. The Sunderland circled above the lifeboat as long as possible, for the sea was too rough for her to land. The Hudson took over the watching brief in the early evening and when it dropped two Thornaby bags near the lifeboat they were successfully recovered by the crew. A note was also dropped indicating that help was on the way. Contact was maintained for two hours in darkness by dropping marine markers. The lifeboat signalled with a torch the word BUCHANAN. Just before 2000 the Hudson, which had been airborne for nearly ten hours, was forced to return to base.

The next day, 21 November, was to be eventful both for the survivors and the searching aircraft. The first officer's lifeboat was re-contacted in the early afternoon by an aircraft of 228 Squadron. HMS *Clare*, also searching in the area, homed on to the aircraft and three hours later a successful rescue was effected. The corvette signalled to the aircraft that there were three more lifeboats in the area, obviously this information came from the rescued first officer.

At much the same time that the first officer's boat had been sighted, another Hudson from 220 Squadron had also sighted a lifeboat while en route to a convoy for escort duties. The Hudson dropped a parachute bag with a Mae West containing emergency rations, signal cartridges and a map giving their position. Nearly two hours later, while still over the lifeboat, the Hudson spotted a Sunderland of 423 Squadron flying some fifteen miles distant. By firing cartridges the Hudson attracted the flying-boat's attention, and the latter took over escort of the boat, which turned out to be the third officer's. HMS *Clare* was again called up and homing on the Sunderland rescued the survivors at 2045.

This left the captain's boat still to be rescued and searches took place on 22 and 23 November to no avail. Interrogation of the survivors established the fact that the lifeboat which had flashed the word 'Buchanan' in perfect morse, to the Hudson on the 20th was probably that of the captain, as he had the ship's radio operator with him. In the afternoon of 24 November another Hudson of 220 Squadron sighted the captain's lifeboat. She was making 2-3 knots steering a course for land. By holding water-containers upside down the occupants demonstrated their need so the Hudson's crew dropped Thornaby bags which included water in tins among other supplies. A second Hudson which, like the first, had covered approximately a thousand miles on the search since leaving land, carried out an interception without the aid of wireless fixes. The position given by the two aircraft differed by only 21 miles. More Thornaby bags were dropped by that aircraft before it set course for base.

At 1930 hours a third Hudson of the squadron arrived on the scene and contacted the patrolling Hudson in the dark with the aid of marine distress markers and relieved this aircraft which returned to base with just thirty gallons of petrol in each tank, after a flight lasting 13½ hours. The relieving aircraft maintained contact by the aid of flares and marine markers until relieved by yet another Hudson at 0315. Three hours later this aircraft homed HMS *Leamington* to the lifeboat. It is interesting to note that ten bearings were obtained on the aircraft by the naval vessel with the result that the latter was able to effect a rescue at 1040 – the lifeboat had been in the sea for thirteen days. A Hudson on the scene was able to signal 'Operation completed 1040 hours – 17 rescued'.

So ended a rescue which had entailed over 30,000 miles of air reconnaissance by aircraft operating from Northern Ireland.

The success of the operation was due to the close and successful co-operation between aircraft and surface vessels – to the persistence and determination of the pilots in continuing their search up to and sometimes beyond their prudent limit of endurance – to the accurate navigation of the searching aircraft and of the surface vessels, and to the efficient plotting and control of Operations by Group Headquarters. It was, above all, a triumph in communications.

The Hudson's crews received congratulations from the Air Officer Commanding Coastal Command, the Admiralty and the Commander-in-Chief Western Approaches.

No doubt the survivors of *Buchanan* would have been cheered by the news that Oberleutnant Hans-Karl Kosbart, commander of *U-224*, was killed two months later when his submarine was sunk by HMCS *Ville de Quebec*.

The fine weather at the end of July 1943 enabled both the Royal Air Force and the United States Army Air Force to undertake a series of raids on Germany. This same fine weather enabled the Air Sea Rescue Hudsons of 279 Squadron, based at Bircham Newton, to assist in the record number of 156 rescues of Allied airmen, of whom 121 were American, from round the shores of the British Isles in the seven day period 25-31 July.

Bomber Command attacked Hamburg on the night of 24 July and this was followed up by a daylight attack by US Flying Fortresses. At the ASR headquarters reports rolled in of distress signals, seen by returning and search aircraft, from the Observer Corps and coastguards; automatic signals on the 500 kilocycle emergency wave length were heard over the ether from dinghy radios. Massive ASR coverage was given and at one time as many as seventy long-range aircraft were in the air at the same time, covering large areas of the North Sea.

Then came the rescues. The Cromer lifeboat reported that it had picked up the crew of a Wellington. This was followed by reports from aircraft that they were orbiting dinghies in five different positions, as far as 200 miles apart. Positions were signalled to HSL's, RML's and other surface craft which were at rescue rendezvous positions, and they were soon on their way. The Cromer lifeboat reported that it had picked up the crew of ten from a Fortress; then came news that a fishing vessel from Sheringham had done likewise. Fighter Command reported that following the sighting of two dinghies twelve miles off Cromer two Walrus aircraft had landed and picked up a further ten American airmen. However, the small amphibian aircraft were unable to take off again with their additional load so the survivors were transferred to a rescue launch that arrived.

In the meantime the squadron commanding officer of No 279 Squadron decided to take an airborne lifeboat himself when a sighting report of a dinghy sixty-five miles from the enemy coast was received. His faithful W-William was only thirty-five miles on the outward track when the crew saw a Fortress which had just ditched in the sea. The American crew were on the wings and climbing into the dinghies. One man appeared unable to move and was clinging to the side of a dinghy.

The skipper decided to drop his lifeboat to this chance-encountered Fortress crew and then return to base, leaving another Hudson over the lifeboat, and send out another boat aircraft to the original sighting position.

The airborne lifeboat alighted successfully 100 yards to one side of the two Fortress dinghies. Drogue and buoyancy equipment worked satisfactorily, fore and aft buoyancy tubes inflated. At 1505, just ten minutes after the drop, the first dinghy load had boarded the lifeboat, which was then paddled over to the second dinghy. The ditched Fortress sank a further ten minutes later leaving a large oil patch The commanding officers wireless operator switched over to 500 k/cs and called up a high speed launch. Three hours later the second Hudson, which was still circling the lifeboat, received a signal by Aldis lamp from the lifeboat :

'Send boat motors' to which was replied :

'Motors under hatch'; the lifeboat answered :

'Motors u/s' to which the aircraft replied :

'Launch on way'.

An Air-Sea rescue Hudson of No 279 Squadron with lifeboat attached.

The lifeboat is dropped only a hundred yards from the dinghy of the crashed Fortress.

The Hudson then sighted the HSL six miles to the south-west and guided it to the lifeboat. The launch picked up the survivors, took the lifeboat in tow at 1915 and landed the airmen at Yarmouth. The aircraft left the scene after the rescue and landed at base just after 2000 having been airborne for nearly six hours.

In the meantime back at Bircham Newton two further Hudsons carrying airborne lifeboats had taken off for the original reported position off the enemy coast. Once again while the Hudsons were on their way to the position they were distracted by pyrotechnics fired by US airmen who were on the sea below in two dinghies tied together. It was decided that one aircraft should stay with these dinghies while the other flew on to the original position. The first Hudson dropped the Lindholme containers and survivors were seen to climb into the dinghy. The Hudson then climbed to get a fix, which was some sixteen miles off Cromer, and signalled a message to base about the dinghy. Two Walrus aircraft arrived in quick succession and took off the survivors.

Meanwhile the lone Hudson resumed course with its radio operator wirelessing back to base 'Continuing search alone'. When nearing the signalled position the Hudson's crew were attracted by a Halifax which led them for some six minutes before they saw another Halifax circling five dinghies, tied together, containing eight US airmen. The Hudson dropped the lifeboat to within thirty yards of the dinghies. Down below, the Americans were startled as they looked upwards for at first they thought that the bottom had fallen out of the twin-engined aircraft: this was not surprising as the Uffa Fox-designed lifeboat covered most of the lower body of the Hudson and only gave minimal ground clearance for the pilot. The survivors paddled a dinghy to the lifeboat which they boarded. They returned to pick up their colleagues. A further signal was sent back to base informing them that the boat had been dropped and the crew were on board. An escort of three Fortresses then arrived and one Halifax left. The survivors were given a course to steer, but later, just as the Hudson was returning to base, the lifeboat was seen to be stationary. A report was received from one of the escorting aircraft that the crew and lifeboat had been picked up and been taken aboard a Danish trawler, fishing off the Dogger Bank. HSL's which had been sent out to intercept them were signalled to get the crew at all costs.

Area Combined Headquarters signalled Hudsons which were searching for the trawlers to persuade the trawler to steer due west.

Hudson O-Orange investigated well over a score of Danish vessels, but no sign was seen of one carrying a lifeboat on its deck. The commanding officer of the squadron who had dropped the first lifeboat the day before, then took up the search, leading a formation of four Hudsons. Less than two hours after take-off, the formation had better luck when the lifeboat was clearly seen on deck of one of the trawlers and the members of the American crew were easily distinguishd on board wearing their bullet-proof vests. A message was flashed to base with the news. Less than an hour later the Hudsons sighted two HSL's nine to ten miles away and one of them guided the rescue boats to the trawler. One of the launches took aboard the American aircrew; the other took charge of the trawler, whose crew were persuaded to continue the journey to England, with the lifeboat still on board. When almost in sight of land the escorting HSL broke down and was towed into Yarmouth next morning by the trawler.

Reports of sightings continued to be received by Flying Control at Area Combined Headquarters, who were organising the searches. HSL's raced to a fresh position and another complete Fortress crew were picked up. Then came a message from an aircraft that another Danish trawler had picked up ten more American airmen from their dinghies, the vessel was found by launches who homed on aircraft circling the trawler, and the crew were taken off.

It was now nearing dusk on the same day – 27 July – when two Spitfire pilots were reported in their dinghies close to the French coast. Out went two Walruses with fighter cover, and both pilots were rescued. Thus in a little over forty-eight hours, since the first SOS had been received, over 100 airmen had been rescued.

From first light on the 28th, the great work continued. A dinghy was sighted and again the lifeboat-carrying Hudson W-William of No 279 Squadron, this time piloted by Flight-Sergeant Palmer, was sent out from Bircham Newton, accompanied by O-Orange. The dinghy was found and the American airmen waved. The lifeboat was successfully dropped just fifty yards from the dinghy, the crew paddled across and were in the lifeboat within five minutes, by which time a message, giving the position had been signalled back to base. The lifeboat's crew were instructed by Aldis lamp to steer a course for home once it was seen that the engines were working. The engines stopped after forty miles and it was in this position that the lifeboat was picked up again next day by the Hudsons of the same squadron. When the lifeboat was found to be stationary, supplies and petrol were dropped by parachute to the occupants who successfully collected them. This was the first time an airborne lifeboat had been refuelled from the air. The crew were soon underway again, but they were lost sight of at least three times by relieving aircraft owing to the very hazy conditions. Although a relieving aircraft failed to relocate the lifeboat, the HSL's which had already been sighted en route to the position, found the lifeboat just before darkness set in, still under its own power, and the entire party docked at Yarmouth late that night.

At midday on the 29th another automatic SOS on 500 kc/s had been received by North Foreland radio station, this tied up with a report that a Fortress of the Fourth Bombardment Wing was in distress about seventy-three miles off Thornaby. Just over two hours later two dinghies containing the ten crew were located by searching aircraft and rescued by a launch. By dusk a further 135 aircraft had searched in the North Sea area alone.

At dawn on 30th, six searches were airborne, carrying on from the previous night's reports. By dusk that evening a further 39 had been rescued, 26 men from the North Sea. Two aircraft out on search from Bircham Newton saw an aircraft ditch, three of the crew were observed making for their dinghy about ten yards away from the aircraft. Four enemy Me210 twin-engined fighters were seen and they made a quick pass at Hudson W-William but did not inflict any damage. Later the same aircraft, this time with a Beaufighter escort, took off on a night search for the crew of the aircraft seen to ditch earlier. Prior to this two No 279 Squadron Hudsons from Harrowbeer took off on separate sorties with Mustang escorts but there was nothing to report. During this day 111 aircraft had been employed in searching the North Sea.

Early on the last day of July three Hudsons kept a rendezvous with eighteen Beaufighters at North Coates before searching for the three airmen in a dinghy. One of the escorts found three K-type and H-type dinghies, containing the three airmen and the airborne lifeboat was successfully dropped and the crew seen to climb aboard. The crew appeared unable to start the engines and therefore hoisted mast and sails and started sailing southwards until a correct course was sent by Aldis lamp.

The closing week of the month proved the value of co-operation between Flying Control at the Air Control headquarters, the USAAF, Bomber and Fighter Command and the Navy. The standard of flying and navigation was high and full use made of ASV radar; it also signified the conclusion of the most active five days in the operational life of No 279 Squadron, which flew 163 operational hours in air/sea rescue sorties.

XV

Around and about Gibraltar

By the spring of 1942 the Hudson had more than proved its worth. There was an increasing demand for the machine at its home in America, from Canada, Australia, New Zealand, and of course, Britain. Twelve months earlier there were 29 long-range Hudsons serving with Coastal Command, they were able to protect shipping up to 250 miles out at sea. Eight Hudsons from both No 206 and No 224 Squadrons were transferred to Aldergrove from Bircham Newton and Leuchars respectively, and a similar number from No 220 Squadron were transferred from Thornabay to Wick, all with the purpose of reinforcing the North-Eastern Approaches.

By the summer of 1941 the production of the ASV radar was becoming more plentiful and fitting parties at Bircham Newton, Wick, Aldergrove and Silloth equipped some 95 Hudsons, mainly with the improved Mark II variation. With the newly fitted equipment, and extra range, the Hudsons were becoming very much in demand and used to their capacity. This led to a situation in mid-1942 when the Chief of the Air Staff was forced to write to the First Sea Lord telling him that his supply of Hudsons would have to be cut.

Sir Charles Portal wrote to Sir Dudley Pound:

> The present commitments of Hudsons exceed the predicted supply from all sources up to the end of 1942 by more than 500 aircraft, therefore there would have to be a reduction of Hudson Squadrons in Coastal Command from 11 to 8.

In fact this was worse than it looked at first sight, as in the existing eleven squadrons there were only 141 aircraft, making a shortage already existing of 79 Hudsons. In the first four-and-a-half months of 1942 Hudsons on anti-shipping operations had sunk five ships totalling some 17,400 tons; during the same time they seriously damaged another fifteen and damaged a further twenty, for a total amounting to over a hundred thousand tons. The Hudsons had paid the price, 29 of them not returning from operations, and it was known that only 13 of these had been lost over the targets. During this time 279 shipping strikes had been carried out, but at the same time over a thousand reconnaissance and off-shore patrols had been covered by Hudsons.

The Germans were well aware of the damage being wrought by the Hudsons and stiffened their defence accordingly. Coastal convoys were now covered by flak ships and this discouraged pilots from attacking too low. Many Ju88's were also encountered at this time. The ships themselves, their R-boat escorts and accompanying minesweepers also had their armaments increased to include 2cm guns and these took their toll of the unfortunate Hudsons, Nos 48, 53, 59, 407 and 608 Squadrons all had their share of losses. As a result of these losses and the shortage of Hudsons, the Norwegian No 330 Squadron that was due to re-equip with Hudsons had to fly Catalina flying-boats instead.

Coastal Command were not the only sufferers due to the shortage of Hudsons. The five meteorological flights with an establishment of thirty were cut down to a dozen, the Central Gunnery School reduced by half to five aircraft and the only then existing Hudson Air-Sea rescue Squadron was reduced from twenty to sixteen aircraft. In all these cases the deficiency was made good by the older Ansons or Oxfords. Of some two hundred troop-carrying Hudsons allocated to the Middle East Command it was recommended that half of these should reconvert to General Reconnaissance machines. The Dominions also had their supply cut back; Australia was cut from 15 to 10 and New Zealand from 9 to 6 aircraft per month.

In the pipeline there was a contract for 469 new Hudsons; of these 52 were Hudson IV's and all were shipped to Australia as part of her quota. The remainder were Mark III and they were divided as follows: The United States claimed some 206 of the Hudsons and allocated 20 to the US Navy, 33 for China and 153 for the Army Air Corps. Of the remaining 211 aircraft, Canada received 104, Australia 49, New Zealand 12, 8 were written off, 5 were seriously damaged and awaiting major refits, 14 were in the hands of the Air Ferry Command, which left only 19 for the United Kingdom.

One of the outcomes of the shortage of Hudsons was that squadrons equipped with the aircraft were now converting to the longer range four-engined American machines that were becoming more plentiful. 206 Squadron followed the example of 220 Squadron and changed to Flying Fortresses while 224 Squadron converted to Liberators.

Despite the Hudson shortages No 500 Coastal Command Squadron was still active; they along with Nos 53, 59 and 608 Squadrons had converted from Blenheims the previous year and in April 1942 moved to Stornaway.

By this time Admiral Karl Dönitz's U-boats were sinking an unacceptable number of merchantmen and it was thought that anti-U-boat patrols would keep them down. For many a Hudson pilot the sighting of an enemy submarine was the high-point of his service career and when there was a sighting, followed by an attack, and photographs of the U-boat on the receiving end, it was an exhilarated crew that returned to base. However, as in claiming an enemy aircraft destroyed, one did not just claim and have a U-boat credited; there was a long procedure before a submarine could be confirmed as sunk. First the report was submitted to the squadron's intelligence officer, then on to the station commander who forwarded on the claim to the U-boat Assessment Committee who had access to all relevant information and upheld or refused the claim. They learned early that the U-boat was very durable, and from information published on U-boat losses since the war it would appear that this Committee did a fine job. A section known as 8s dealt with U-boat traffic.

One of the first attacks by a 500 Squadron pilot took place on 28 April when Flight Sergeant Higginbotham flew K-King from Stornaway on the late afternoon in fair weather over a moderate sea. A precis of the attack was submitted :

The Hudson was flying on an A/S patrol at a height of 4,000 feet and sighted a U-boat on the surface at a range of 7-8 miles. The U-boat was steering 250 degrees. The Hudson approached apparently without being seen, and attacked with a stick of four 250 lb depth charges, spaced 60 feet apart. The U-boat was still on the surface at the time of the attack and was straddled by the first two depth charges of the stick. The pilot considers that complete surprise was achieved due to the rapid descent of the aircraft and it is stated that three of the U-boat's crew were actually in the conning tower when the depth charges were released. The explosions of the depth charges blew the U-boat's bows clear of the water, and the submarine appeared to slide back stern first at an angle of about twenty degrees. The U-boat's bows re-appeared with an apparent list to starboard before finally disappearing in a large patch of frothy brown water.

Meanwhile, after pulling out of her dive, the Hudson had turned and passed over the U-boat again attacking it with front and turret guns. Hits were observed on the bows and conning tower. The Hudson remained in the vicinity for fifty minutes but nothing further was seen. The U-boat was described as a large one with wire cutters on its bows. It was painted light grey but the inside of the coning tower was red – guns were not observed.

The station commander remorked : 'A skilful attack, the result of which, in my opinion, fully justified a claim that the U-boat was destroyed.'

The submarine tracking room's opinion was : 'Tracking evidence is inconclusive, but it appears unlikely that this U-boat made any signals within 36 hours of the attack.'

The decision of the U-boat assessment committee was : 'The committee are hopeful that some future evidence will show that this U-boat was in fact sunk, but for the present are unable to assess it higher than "Probably damaged A." ' This result of the Assessment Committee was published three weeks after the attack and post-war German records show that the submarine was not sunk.

Two other pilots serving with 500 Squadron at this time were New Zealanders Ian Patterson and Michael Ensor. We have already met Ian and will do so again shortly. After leaving school Michael Ensor attempted to join the RAF on a short service commission when war broke out but was not immediately accepted for training. He worked at his father's sheep farm in Rangiora until his turn came to enrol. After arriving in England and following his training at an OTU he quickly progressed to join 500 Squadron.

In January 1942 he piloted his aircraft, one of three, toward the enemy coast at Heligoland in clear moonlight. Two-and-a-half hours after take off he saw three small supply ships and attacked at mast-height, bombing the leading ship. Immediately after this there followed an incident that was to win him the DFC – he takes up the story himself :

We continued our patrol. We were now in Heligoland Bight and flying towards the mouth of the Elbe. Searchlights flicked up at us, and one held us for a time. We were flying at about a hundred feet, and it was then that we hit a rock. None of us saw it. There was a terrific dull, grinding crash, and the aircraft bounced up a good many feet.

The airscrews of the starboard engine were bent right back over the cowling, and the motor was badly knocked about, so I switched it off. Then I noticed that the airspeed indicator was not working, and the wireless went out of action. I climbed to about 1,000 feet and set a course for home on the gyro-compass. I didn't find out until we were over Holland that it was 180 degrees out. I was having difficulty in flying the aircraft without the airspeed indicator.

The Germans started to send up flak at us, and we had to fly further inland and get down to hedge-hopping level. My observer got in the nose and told me when to climb to avoid trees and buildings and ack-ack batteries. The flak was fairly intense. It was as though somebody was spraying red sparks at us from a giant hose-pipe. That went on for about half-an-hour, and once we narrowly missed hitting a wireless station.

Eventually, we got out to sea again, but we could not be sure of the direction we were taking; but I steered on the magnetic compass, and when we landed we were only twenty miles off our course. It took us two-and-a-half hours to get back, and once we ran into a heavy snow storm. We flew through it for an hour. It was pitch dark, and we could hardly see the wing-tips. If we shone a torch we could see the snow streaking past like black lines made by a number of pencils.

We had just got down to our last half-hour's petrol when we saw land, so I decided to come down. It was still dark and difficult to pick out a suitable field. We flew around for a time, letting off Very lights to help us find an acceptable spot. Our lighting system and landing lights were out of action, and it was pretty difficult.

Eventually, however, I managed to get her down to a belly landing in a field studded with poles – anti-invasion poles for the Jerries to hit if they tried landing. We struck a couple, but I got her down all right. My observer was the only one who got injured. He collected a black eye and had a tooth knocked out. I think we found about the only spot in England where it was not snowing at that moment.

Everyone was surprised to see us when we got back to the station. After our wireless set packed up they hadn't heard from us. They thought we'd gone for a burton.

On 6 July Ensor attacked a U-boat on the surface; the bows were blown out of the water but it survived. Towards the end of August he attacked another surfaced U-boat, his depth charges burst across the bows but not within the lethal twenty feet necessary for the kill.

One point a Hudson pilot had to consider in regard to the aiming mark in an 'up the track' attack was that owing to the forward travel of bombs or depth-charges under water, the whole stick moved forward some forty feet after impact and before detonation. If the average length of a stick was taken as 150 feet the first depth-charge was aimed to fall on the leading edge of the swirl as the submarine dived, the last one would actually explode 150 plus 40, or 190 feet ahead of the swirl. In other words the pilot could aim his first charge at the leading edge of the swirl up to fifteen seconds after submergence and still get one depth-charge within lethal range. No doubt Michael Ensor had learned from his U-boat attacks. In fact he was awarded a bar to his DFC for his efforts in the North Atlantic; in all he attacked four U-boats in that zone of operations although none was sunk.

In early November Rommel's Afrika Korps were in full retreat and it was thought that the forthcoming 'Operation Torch', the landing of Allied troops on the North African coast would attract an unusual amount of attention from U-boats. No 500 Squadron therefore moved to Gibraltar.

Gibraltar at this time was a military stronghold. The civilian population had been evacuated in May 1940 when the Germans started their offensive in Northern Europe. Some 15,000 Gibraltarians were evacuated from the Rock to the West Indies, the Canary Islands and England. Some of the children were billeted in the Kensington district of London; this could hardly have been safer than the Rock!

As had been realised from the time Sir George Rooke secured Gibraltar for Britain with an Anglo-Dutch force in 1704, the Rock was strategically placed at the entrance to the Mediterranean and it is doubtful whether the forthcoming North African landings could have been as successful without the land-based aircraft that were to operate from its airstrip. Before the war the Bay had been used for RAF flying-boats and discussions about the construction of a military airstrip had been going on between the services and the Foreign Office during the thirties. The only possible place to construct an airfield was at the base of the Rock, at almost sea level and hard against the Spanish border.

At the time the belief was that France would be Britain's ally, and the use of airfields in France would be sufficient to obtain air mastery over the Mediterranean. The strip of land that was required for the airstrip covered the old neutral ground between Spain and Gibraltar; this had been converted to a racecourse and a military training ground. Prior to the war only light civilian planes had landed at Gibraltar, with the military flying boats landing in the bay.

After the fall of France a good deal more thought was given to the construction of a large scale military airfield near the Rock. During the early part of the century thousands of tons of rock were blasted from Sandy Bay to construct the harbour. Now thousands more tons of rock, stone and rubble were being excavated as tunnels were constructed to provide accommodation for living, sleeping and hospital facilities for the garrison as well as communication tunnels. With the surplus rock being excavated a decision was required on where to dump it; the obvious answer was in the Bay of Algeciras, and this formed the base for the airstrip that was to extend half-a-mile into the Bay. This was a major engineering feat and while sappers were busy at their work their opposite numbers on the diplomatic side were busy talking with Franco's Spanish Government whose sympathies at this time were strongly pro-German although officially neutral.

The work on the airfield construction continued apace, only the very top military people were in the know about its importance for the forthcoming North African invasion. As well as its aircraft giving the soldiers and fleet air cover, its use as a base for anti-submarine strikes was obvious. If a large concentration of shipping was to be used to convey Allied troops to Algeria, its presence would attract U-boats as a moth to a flame. And so the work progressed, the runway continued with stone being rolled into the ground at an astonishing rate, so much so that when it was lengthened to 1,150 yards in April 1942 Hudsons from Nos 233, 500 and 608 Squadrons were able to fly out from the United Kingdom and land there while the runway was still being extended out to sea. Then, as now, there was always a danger of being blown against the face of the Rock when landing in a cross wind.

A major difficulty in operating the airfield was that the labour force of Spanish workers from La Linea had to cross the airfield twice each day on their way to work in Gibraltar. Among these workers the Germans found it easy to infiltrate intelligence agents, and it was probably for this reason that when General Eisenhower, who was chosen to lead the Allied Expeditionary Force for Operation Torch, arrived he was accommodated underground in Gibraltar, which was not very much to his liking.

Many of the local difficulties had been settled by the time Flying

Officer Ensor, and I emphasise his rank because by a strange co-incidence his squadron leader was also named Ensor – flew his faithful white-painted Hudson MK–S from Portreath direct to Gibraltar on 5 November 1942. At this time immediately prior to the landings, he, and the rest of 500 Squadron who had also recently arrived at the Rock, was quartered in Nissen huts. The living conditions suffered somewhat from overcrowding as there was an enormous number of flying personnel stationed there. No one minded as there was obviously something big in the wind and the squadron was in the forefront of the battle.

After the landings, Ensor and some of the other pilots were sent to Tafouri on detachment. One Hudson was detailed to convey General Giraud who took command of the French North African Forces to Blida Airport near Algiers. The aircraft was a gift to the General and arrived painted in French colours escorted by six Spitfires.

The detachment at Tafouri all slept on hangar floors; the aircrew were without any covering except that afforded by their flying clothing.

On 15 November five Hudsons took off on a parallel search for U-boats. The previous day *U-595* had been sunk in the area – the first by 500 Squadron Hudsons.

Michael Ensor took off at 0850 in the aircraft he had brought out from England. Although he did not know it at the time, it was to be his last operational sortie flying a Hudson. The aircraft had been airborne nearly four hours and was flying at 7,000 feet some sixty miles north of Algiers when suddenly Ensor saw a shape resembling a cigar on the blue Mediterranean.

Down below the U-boat spotted the Hudson at much the same time. Kapitänleutnant Klaus Köpice, the commanding officer of *U-259*, a Type VIIC boat, had to make a quick decision. He could stay on the surface and fight or make an immediate crash-dive. There was really no option, for the Hudson would be upon the submarine before it had fully submerged. He ordered his crew to man the guns.

The pilot called excitedly over the inter-com as he swung the Hudson into a right-angle dive. Looking out from the aircraft, the crew could see the Germans at their anti-aircraft gun. Their commander was exhorting them to fire, but by the time the Hudson was over the U-boat no shots had been fired.

The Hudson pulled out of its dive and at fifty feet the depth-charges went spinning down to their target. As the aircraft pulled away it was blown upwards. The second of the four depth-charges had scored a direct hit and must have exploded a torpedo or the magazine. In the enormous explosion that followed the U-boat's gun was flung into the air and the conning tower was ripped open.

This 'dry-hit' sent the Hudson rocketing nearly 500 feet, it had received the full upward thrust, the turret and cabin floor were blown in, all windows were broken and all movable equipment was uprooted. When the pilot recovered consciousness he found broken perspex from his cabin window lying in his lap. As he quickly came to, he realised that the Hudson was now diving steeply and that he must do something quickly to arrest the dive. He grabbed the control column and pulled for all he was worth, for the sea below was getting ominously close. The Hudson did not respond, so he put the airscrews into fine pitch and jammed the throttles forward as far as they would go. Slowly, but so slowly, the nose of the faithful Hudson rose. They were on even keel again, but it was obvious that something was badly wrong with the aircraft.

The rear-gunner shouted over the inter-com, 'Skipper, you've lost your elevator, and both rudders are just hanging on by their bloody hinges.'

Looking round, Ensor discovered that the wings were pointing upwards, the port wing tip was almost at right angles. He eased the controls forward, but by now the Hudson was labouring, and the engines causing vibration. The Hudson was not answering the controls, so he decided to get the weight in the forward part of the aircraft and called the crew to his cabin. With the redistribution of weight the engines began to purr more evenly and the nose dipped. The Hudson was flying straight and level at 1,000 feet although Ensor discovered the controls were still not answering properly. The nearest coastline was Algiers and it was obviously the place to make for, since the crew knew the reputation of Hudsons landing on the sea.

The only way the pilot could get the Hudson pointing in the right direction was by alternating the speed of the engines. By getting the crew to walk backward and forward, keeping his left hand on the throttles Ensor was able to coax the aircraft up to 3,000 feet. As a safety measure the crew were told to fetch their parachutes. The navigator's parachute had been buried in the nose, under other equipment, by the force of the explosion. As he went forward to retrieve it the nose again dipped and the aircraft was almost at sea level before he was able to crawl back with it. By now the engines were really in a bad way and labouring. Despite the pilot giving full boost and revs the Hudson was only making about 100 miles per hour, only just above stalling speed, and the dangers of this happening had been drilled into all Hudson pilots.

There was relief when the coast of Algiers was suddenly sighted. The altimeter again registered 1,000 feet; to get it to climb at all Ensor had to close the engine cooling gills and it was this that caused one of the motors to cough and suddenly cut out without any warning. Immediately the Hudson went into a spin. It was now time to get out, and quickly!

The navigator, bomb-aimer and the rear-gunner all jumped before the pilot. Ensor's parachute had only just opened when he hit the water, for they were still just over the sea. Hurriedly, he released his harness, at the same time he saw his Hudson crash into the water.

Help was soon at hand when a Royal Navy sloop picked him up. His rear-gunner was also saved but the other two members of the crew were found dead. One of the crew was knocked unconscious when he hit the fuselage as he jumped and was drowned; the other's parachute failed to open.

The jubilation at headquarters was tempered by the loss of two of the most experienced and popular members of the squadron. Needless to say, *U-259* was a total loss.

After only seventeen days in Gibraltar Flying Officer Ensor, who was awarded a DSO for the U-boat success, flew Hudson X-ray back to the UK for repairs and remained on the staff of Coastal Command Headquarters for six months. Later, after converting to Liberators, he won quick promotion and by January 1944 when still only twenty-three years of age was a wing commander with a bar to his DSO.

Before going on to the story of Ian Patterson's greatest success I feel it is necessary here to describe the U-boat's conning tower look-out procedure.

The bridge watch consisted of four men, the officer of the watch covering port 90 degrees to right astern, one seaman port 90 degrees to right ahead, one petty officer of the watch right ahead to starboard 90 degrees and one seaman starboard 90 degrees to right astern. All were issued with binoculars and anti-dazzle glasses. Watch-keeping on the bridge was a fatiguing and exacting task, yet at all times the men had to be alert. Visual sighting was the key. With the noise of the diesels, the look-outs could not hear the sound of approaching aircraft; this was known and made use of by Coastal Command aircraft. If an

No 500 Squadron Z-Zebra with which Ian Patterson (*inset*) made the attack on
U-331 (*below*).

enemy was sighted an electric bell gave the alarm; the petty officer of the watch went below to his action station in the conning-tower with the commanding officer. The starboard quarter look-out went to the after hydroplanes and the officer of the watch was the last below. It was his duty to remove the aerial and to close the hatch. He then went to his action station in the control-room. The responsibility for choosing between diving and fighting lay with the officer of the watch. It was recommended that the U-boat should dive if it sighted the aircraft in good time to avoid a 'surprise attack', that is one in which the aircraft approached to within 2,000–3,000 metres without being sighted, in which case the U-boat was encouraged to fight it out on the surface.

We already know Ian Patterson's record with the Hudson since September 1939 and of his flying the first Fortress to cross the Atlantic, but in 1936, when he was a nineteen-year-old electrical engineering apprentice in Auckland his heart was more set on aerodynamics than on volts and amperes. When the *New Zealand Herald* sponsored a contest for a course of flying lessons at Mangere aerodrome, he could not wait to fill out his application form.

'Quite a crowd of air-minded young chaps turned up for the contest,' he recalls. 'We had to answer questions about aircraft and aviation in general.' The young Patterson did not win that contest but the experience spurred him on to save every penny of his meagre cash and pay for a course of flying lessons.

Having obtained his pilot's licence, he joined the RNZAF as a trainee airman, 'and there were precious few in those days', won his pilot-officer's wings and then applied for a commission in the Royal Air Force.

He had been with the RAF in England six months when war broke out, now three years later he was a squadron leader with No 500 Squadron. He too had moved over from Gibraltar with the Tafouri detachment and it was from that airfield, near Oran, that he gently lifted his Hudson AM714, Z-Zebra, out on an anti-submarine patrol at 0800 on 17 November.

Soon he was over the Mediterranean, sparkling blue in the winter sunlight, no doubt reflecting how fortunate the squadron had been in sinking two U-boats in two days. He had been airborne for an hour-and-a-half when his reflections were cut short, as down below, travelling westward at a leisurely 12 knots, he spotted the wake of a submarine. The sea was calm and the visibility extreme. The pilot knew that an attack from down-sun would be useless with the prevailing degree of visibility, and endeavoured to work around until he was up-sun. But despite the application of every wile learned in the hard months of training, and practised assiduously, he was seen from the U-boat.

The U-boat below was no ordinary U-boat. It was captained by an ace, Hans Dietrich Freiherr von Tiesenhausen, who twelve months earlier had sunk *HMS Barham* in what Admiral Cunningham, Commander-in-Chief Mediterranean, had described as 'a most daring and brilliant attack'!

It was at 1100 on 7 November that *U-331* left from Bassin No 1 at La Spezia on its ninth and last patrol. The morale on board was good, the crew proud to serve under a commander who had won the *Ritter-kreuz* for his great achievement. Tiesenhausen placed great emphasis on the importance of efficient watch-keeping, in view of the great danger from aircraft in the Mediterranean. With this end in view, he did his best to retain those men with whom he had got to know and to trust. Despite this, the Drafting Depot at the Italian port insisted on fourteen ratings being embarked before sailing, twelve to replace old hands required elsewhere, and two as supernumeraries for experience. The result was that many of the ratings were altogether without experience of U-boats.

It had originally been intended that *U-331* should sail about 15 November but the sailing date was advanced when news of the Allied landings in North Africa was received. Before sailing, the commander told his men that Hitler had sent to Captain (S) Mediterranean a signal of the 'do or die' variety to be issued to all boats.

The operational area of the U-boat was to be in the neighbourhood of Algiers and after leaving La Spezia *U-331* sailed north of Corsica and then south at full speed on the surface. The next day the US army transport *Leedstown* of over 9,000 tons was torpedoed in a bay east of Cape Matafou by a salvo of four angled torpedoes. The same day the U-boat commander sighted some escorted aircraft carriers but was unable to attack owing to the high speed and zig-zagging of the formation and later that same evening an escorted troop transport was seen making for Gibraltar but the submarine could not overhaul her owing to her speed. On 13 November *U-331* surfaced to send signals but was spotted by destroyers and depth-charged but escaped.

On the night of 15/16 a destroyer was sighted but no action resulted. On the 17th the U-boat was proceeding westward at periscope depth north-west of Algiers. There was no sign of enemy activity and the commander gave the order to surface, and the boat continued at slow speed westward. The search receiver was not in position, as during the day-time the crew relied more on visual than other methods for spotting aircraft.It was usually the officer of the watch's duty to mount the equipment in position.

After the U-boat surfaced, an aircraft was spotted flying eastwards on the port bow. As it was some considerable distance away it was thought that it would not see the U-boat, but, when it turned towards it, the U-boat immediately dived. No attack was heard, so two hours later Tiesenhausen surfaced to periscope depth and, as there was no sign of the enemy, he gave the order to fully surface.

This was exactly the move Ian Patterson had been waiting for, everything was working to plan. After the first sighting, he decided his only hope was to 'bait' his quarry. This entailed flying eastwards and up-sun for nearly 100 miles and climbing to a height where white camouflage could be most effective – 10,000 feet on such a day. Returning to the U-boat's last seen position two hours later, he was rewarded by the sight, through binoculars, of a wake, which could only mean one thing.

Warning the crew that the target was in sight, he began a long dive, overcoming the difficulty of reducing the speed as much as possible by flattening the pitch of the airscrews. One mistake was made, not opening the bomb door until half-way down, at maximum speed, which seriously upset the trim of the aircraft, but when completed, helped to keep the needle below the red line.

On the U-boat the starboard quarter lookout did not see the air-craft. The port quarter look-out, on his first operational patrol, saw it too late and it was the commander himself who sounded the alarm which started the U-boat diving.

For the pilot of the attacking Hudson everything was working well; within a thousand yards of the U-boat, he reduced height to 20 feet and, just before the Hudson lifted over the conning tower, four Mark XI Torpex depth charges set to shallow depth and spaced 35 feet apart were released. Three straddled the target and the fourth-hung-up.

Tiesenhausen suffered from shock after the explosions, and in the confusion that followed was under the impression that one of his crew was wounded by machine-gun fire. This was not so because the attack-ing aircraft did not fire on the run-up.

The 88 mm gun was put out of action and the forward hatch burst open and jammed. This led to water entering the forward compartment, which the commander then ordered to be cleared and the forward watertight bulkhead closed. The diesels were also damaged and one battery put out of action. Tiesenhausen then switched over to the other battery and continued ahead as fast as possible. The pressure hull was still undamaged.

Patterson claimed that the stick straddled, exploding on each side of the U-boat and lifting her up in the water. Tiesenhausen was under the impression that three bombs only were dropped and that they exploded fifteen yards distant to port. He at once ordered the crew to put on life-jackets in case a larger scale attack developed, necessitating abandoning ship.

The Hudson pulled round steeply to port, and passing over the U-boat again, machine-gunned the decks in an effort to saturate any attempt to man the guns. It then climbed to 1,000 feet and sent off a signal reporting the attack. Two further Hudsons then appeared. These were L-Lucy and C-Charlie both of No 500 Squadron. Attacking from the U-boat's starboard quarter at 60 degrees to track, from a height of 50 feet, L-Lucy released four Mark XI Torpex depth-charges set to shallow depth and spaced 36 feet apart. The pilot stated that No 1 depth-charge exploded on the starboard side, No 2 against the port side and Nos 3 and 4 over on the port side. When spray subsided, the U-boat remained stationary on the surface. This attack wrecked all the depth-gauges and compasses and put the steering out of order, so that *U-331* inclined to circle.

The U-boat commander then ordered all men not on duty below on to the upper deck, in case it should be necessary to abandon ship.

The remaining aircraft now dropped a further three Mark XI Torpex depth-charges released from a height of 50 feet in an attack made from the U-boat's port quarter at 60 degrees to track. The depth-charges were set at shallow depth and spaced about 36 feet apart. At this point the U-boat was fully surfaced and several of the crew were seen on the bridge. The No 4 depth-charge failed to release. This stick straddled the U-boat and explosions were seen on either side of the conning-tower. After the spray had settled some of the crew, presumably those who had been on the bridge, were seen in the water. The U-boat was still on the surface and stopped. The depth-charges dropped in this attack blasted a number of those on deck overboard and killed a crew member. These two attacking aircraft then set course for base.

At this point a serious attempt was made to man the guns but those who tried were either cut down by machine-gun fire from the Hudson, or jumped overboard to avoid it. Each time the aircraft approached and swept the conning tower more men fell to the guns of the attacker, and the deck became red with blood. A number of the crew came up from below, and waiting until Z-Zebra had finished a run, donned life-jackets and began swimming away from their crippled boat. The pilot, thinking that an attempt was being made to scuttle *U-331*, dropped a 100 lb A/S bomb, instantaneously fused, among them, and those that survived returned to the submarine. By this time Ian Patterson was having difficulty with a smoke-blackened windscreen, and most of the ammunition in the Hudson had been expended. As a last effort the Hudson pilot started a climb to carry out a dive-bombing attack with the one remaining 100 lb bomb.

Below, with his U-boat totally unable to dive with the forward hatch open and no chance of being able to cover it, the submarine commander ordered a white flag to be hoisted on humanitarian grounds to save the loss of further lives to his crew.

The Hudson acknowledged this sign and the crew took stock of the situation. Fuel was running low and calculated insufficient to take the aircraft right back to base. Signals had been sent requesting assistance with the U-boat but no shipping could be seen in the vicinity. The nearest airfield was Maison Blanche, Algiers, so the navigator set course for there. On arrival Ian Patterson spoke by telephone to the Navy giving the exact position of *U-331* He was informed that a destroyer, HMS *Wilton,* was being despatched and he stated that as soon as his aircraft had been refuelled and re-armed he would return to the U-boat and guide the ship to the spot.

Concurrently, those remaining on board *U-331* had been making efforts to rescue their shipmates swimming in the water. By this time, as a result of the flooding of the forward compartment, the submarine was down by the bows to the extent that her screws were practically out of the water. The commander gave the order to go astern on the motors, realising that this would be their only chance of escape.

Meanwhile, the engine-room personnel had managed to repair the diesels so that they could be made to function at slow speed. The U-boat therefore proceeded very slowly towards the North African coast, estimated by the commander to be about twelve miles distant, partly on her diesels and partly on her motors. The aim in proceeding astern towards the coast was not so much to save their lives as to make land

and escape. Tiesenhausen said that it was hopeless to proceed to sea as he was already so close to the coast and could not submerge. The U-boat captain then ordered *U-331* to be prepared for sinking and destroyed all secret documents and made an open signal describing his position.

The submarine then abandoned all attempts to make land, as the propellers were practically exposed. The ship's company tended their wounded and *U-331* remained stopped. Some of the men tried to make rafts out of sections of the deck covering, their rubber dinghies having been destroyed by blast from the depth-charges.

Elsewhere in the Mediterranean the signal from Z-Zebra about the U-boat surrendering was having effect. It was picked up by the aircraft carrier HMS *Formidable* and she at once despatched a striking force consisting of three Albacore biplanes and an escort of Grumman Martlet fighters to the scene. When they arrived the Hudson was back guarding her prize and *Wilton* was about eight miles away. The presence of these aircraft gave cause for alarm to Ian Patterson as, everything being under perfect control, he was afraid that they might attack. To ward off this possibility he endeavoured to keep his aircraft between the U-boat and the new arrivals, and by every means possible warn them that their help was not needed. Nevertheless, a Martlet dived on the men waving white flags and machine-gunned the decks from bow to stern. The gunfire penetrated *U-331*'s conning tower killing some and wounding others. Tiesenhausen and his Second Lieutenant were both wounded. One of the Albacores then penetrated the Hudson's 'screen' and from 700 yards dropped an 18 inch torpedo, Mark XII, duplex pistol, set to 12 feet, speed 40 knots. The torpedo track was clearly evident and Tiesenhausen ordered hard-a-starboard on the hand operated rudder, but it was too late. The ensuing explosion nearly hit the Hudson which was almost immediately overhead, some of the pieces and crew of *U-331* being above it, in the air.

The torpedo struck *U-331* on the starboard side, killing 32 men who were still below; the remainder were thrown into the water. A second explosion was observed under water and wreckage was seen.

The attacks by the Martlet and the Albacore were observed from *Wilton* but she was too far away to prevent them. A Walrus flying-boat then appeared on the scene, picked up the survivors, about nine in number, endeavoured to take off but found that her cargo was too heavy. She accordingly put some of the men back in the water and took off with the remainder. Those left swimming were then picked up by

Wilton which continued searching for a long period for further survivors, but found none.

Ian Patterson and his crew in Z-Zebra were disgusted at what had happened and left the scene while the destroyer was searching for further survivors.

Ian Patterson was later awarded the DSO and the citation mentioned the attack. A signal was sent from the Admiralty which read:

Request you convey the congratulations of their Lordships to No 500 (GR) Squadron on the successful destruction of three U-boats on the 14, 15 and 17 November.

Added at the end of the signal was another from the Eastern Air Command which said:

This is high and well deserved praise. The work of the squadron entailing long hours of flying over the sea can be, at times, extremely tedious. It is, however, vital and I am glad it has been crowned with success and I know that more will come.

Squadron Leader Patterson was awarded his decoration early in 1943, in the meantime the Albacore pilot was court-martialled for having torpedoed *U-331* while it was flying the white flag.

Two weeks after the attack when home on leave in London Ian Patterson was invited by Admiralty Intelligence officers to meet Baron von Tiesenhausen, who had been among the 17 survivors. The New Zealander says: 'The German was extremely cold and hostile, he told me straight out that he blamed me for the cold-blooded and brutal destruction of his ship and crew.' Nothing could convince the German of the pilot's innocence and Patterson hastily terminated the interview. While Ian Patterson was enjoying a well-earned spot of leave in London another Hudson pilot on a transit flight to Gibraltar was encountering similar conditions experienced by Jim Pedersen two-and-a-half years earlier. He recalls his experience of flying through cumulonimbus cloud with violent air currents and electrical disturbances:

'I had made the same trip from the United Kingdom several times and knew the route by sight. This, together with 1,100 hours operations, and a total of 1,400 hours on this type of aircraft, inclined me to be a bit over-confident about the flight.

'We started about 0200 hours so as to arrive early in the morning. Right at the start I began to climb the Hudson and be above any ice as well as assisting the astro navigation, and making a good air speed. We finally levelled out at 12,000 feet, well in the clear. Everything was too perfect.

'About three hours out, the thought of coffee and sandwiches lured me away from the controls, and the second pilot, a spare body, took over. He released the automatic pilot and was doing the flying himself. As he was a new lad out of an Operational Training Unit and it was the first time I had seen him fly I watched him for about ten minutes and was happy about his ability.

'At 0630 the engines were purring beautifully. My mind had already completed the trip, and I was contemplating the pleasant process of peeling a banana. Just then I noticed that a great black wall had cut out the stars. It was certain that we would encounter icing, once we were in it, so the carburettor heaters were put in and de-icing equipment checked. The stuff was too high to go over and it seemed a bit hopeless to try to go round. The only thing to do was a quick descent.

'We were in the cloud only a few minutes when the ice began to form. It was not heavy, and it kept breaking off in thin sheets. At about 7,000 feet we entered cloud, which seemed more turbulent than what we had met before. It was then that blue flames, six to eight inches long began leaping from the wing-tips, aerials, and propellers. The aircraft began to drop rapidly, and hit bumps which were making the altimeter jump up and down two to three hundred feet.

'The rest of the crew had never before seen St Elmo's fire, and the pilot, who had been doing such a good job on the instrument flying, was gaping with open mouth at the beautiful little lights on the wing-tips. I made some short, rude remarks, which had the desired effect, and he carried on the business of clock watching.

'Then there came a short calm. At this time we were flying at 4,500 feet so we swopped seats rapidly. He carried out a check to see that all the wireless was off, and the trailing aerial in. It so happened that the wireless operator had already taken this action.

'Suddenly the bumps began again. This time we were going up at a terrific rate. If the first time had been bad, it was a pram ride compared to this. The St Elmo's fire had increased until the flames were jumping two to three feet on the wing-tips and aerials. The propellers were two great discs of fire, like the fire wheels one sees on Guy Fawkes night, only on a much greater scale. It was raining hard and the water drops, which partially froze as they hit the aircraft, were little balls of fire. They made the windscreen look like a solid sheet of flame. The whole aircraft was glowing with the weird blue light. We were all so astounded by the amazing phenomena that the fact that I had throttled well back, and we were being thrown all over the sky, despite desperate wrestling with the controls, did not seem to penetrate my mind. The nose was at an alarming angle, according to the artificial horizon and the rate of climb indicator. The altimeter at this time was reading 8,500 feet. All the time it felt as if some giant hand was shoving the aircraft one way and then another. Probably the whole thing did not last more than three or four minutes, but it seemed like ages.

'After coming into another down draught and levelling out at 2,000 feet, I decided that it would be best to stay low.

'It didn't seem long afterwards when dawn broke. Then everyone settled down to the rest of the flight with a feeling of relief. I do remember in the middle of it all that I made a mental promise to take back all the rude and sharp words I had previously said to my co-pilot. The wireless operator had cut his hands holding on to something to keep from hitting the roof. A most remarkable thing was that during the worst of it, the co-pilot had somehow managed to fasten my harness, and fasten himself down at the same time. It is an easy thing to think of it later, but for anyone who does not appreciate the difficulties he had, I might add that it was a feat of strength, acrobatics, and all-in wrestling combined.

'The remainder of the trip was quite normal. The only special precaution necessary was to see that the aircraft was well grounded after landing, although the tail wheel is normally a good conductor of electricity.

'This little episode is not the most scaring that came my way: but I can truthfully say that it was certainly the most startling. It gave me the busiest five minutes I have ever spent in the air. I am glad it happened, because if ever I meet one of those nasty black clouds again I shall certainly recognise it and climb over or go under it.'

Moving into 1943 the Hudson aircraft in and around Gibraltar continued to harry U-boats that dared to show themselves. On 12 February Hudson F-Freddie of No 48 Squadron sank *U-442* off Portugal and on 4 March V-Victor of No 500 Squadron sank *U-83*. On 28 March Hudsons from Nos 48 and 233 Squadrons combined to sink *U-77* and

A Hudson 111 leaves the packed dispersal park at Gibraltar in August 1942.

A Hudson of No 500 Squadron piloted by F/Lt Barwood DFC.

on 5 April two Hudsons from No 233 Squadron sank *U-167* off the Canary Islands.

May 1943 was the turning point for the U-boats. Admiral Dönitz had confidently sent his U-boat fleet back into battle after their great convoy successes in March, but by the time the month ended they had been pulled out of line as 41 of his submarines had been sunk by various means. Two were sunk by Mediterranean-based Hudsons.

In the early evening of 7 May Sergeant 'Dutchy' Holland was flying Hudson X-ray of No 233 Squadron on what at first sight appeared to be a routine anti-submarine patrol. He was at 3,500 feet in 5/10 cloud which had a base of 5,000 feet. Down below the sea was blue and smooth and although visibility was fifteen miles, the low sun hampered vision to the west. A vessel was sighted on the starboard side seven miles distant and as the aircraft closed, it was seen to be a U-boat making about five knots. By this time the Hudson was just four miles off and as there was visual contact the radar was switched off in case the submarine was picking up its transmission.

The twin-engined aircraft, with the distinctive silhouette, descended and on the approach took evasive action, finally attacking from the U-boat's starboard bow at sixty degrees to track, releasing from 50–70 feet four Mark XI Torpex depth-charges, set to shallow depth, spaced 100 feet, while the U-boat was still on the surface. Evidence showed that the depth-charge on the starboard side was fifteen yards from the hull and the one on the port side was ten yards from the hull. A piece of debris, thrown into the air by the explosions was seen by the rear gunner who was firing at the time and so was unable to observe any details. Four or five men were seen in the conning-tower, looking at the aircraft as it passed over, and two men were standing next to the forward gun but they made no attempt to fire. The U-boat appeared to be lifted bodily by the explosions and then it settled down into the water.

After the attack the aircraft turned and the U-boat was seen, still with its helm on, moving very slowly and blowing its tanks. The aircraft then sighted another No 233 Squadron Hudson circling the U-boat. Doubtful as to what the other Hudson was doing, X-ray tried to signal her; it had no effect and nor did the Aldis flashing light. The attacking Hudson remained in the vicinity for forty minutes before making for base when the prudent limit of endurance had been reached and flew in over the Bay of Algeciras and landed at Gibraltar.

The final evidence the crew were waiting for was supplied the following morning when a No 48 Squadron aircraft reported a large oil patch in the same position. The U-boat, which was *U-447*, under the command of veteran submariner, newly promoted Kapitänleutnant Friedrich Bothe, had been sunk before it had time to attack any Allied shipping.

Towards the end of February Hudsons .from No 608 Squadron moved over to the airfield at Blida in Algeria, preparatory to starting operations. Later in that same month another event occurred which boded no good for the enemy's underwater attackers; the U-boat Warfare Committee told the Cabinet that Coastal Command Headquarters had reported the successful completion of trials with rocket-projectiles fitted to both Beaufighters and Hudsons.

The weather was fine on the morning of Friday, 28 May when Flying-Officer G. A. K. Ogilvie, with Flying-Officer J. L. J. Tester as navigator, lifted his Hudson M-Mary off the airfield for a U-boat strike. There were forty-five minutes of the morning left as the dumpy aircraft climbed into the cloudless blue sky and shortly afterwards was on track flying northwards over the Mediterranean which was covered by a heat haze shimmering over the clear blue sea. The aircraft was newly fitted with the rocket-rails, one under each wing, all that was wanted now was an obliging U-boat to test the projectiles on. An object was sighted on the water below, but as the pilot descended to investigate, it was seen to be a square-shaped barge, larger than a landing barge, loaded with timber or people. To the north of the Balearic Islands, which were carefully skirted as Spain was neutral, after nearly two hours in the air, while flying at 4,000 feet in nil cloud a U-boat was sighted on the surface on the port side some eight miles distant travelling at about twelve knots.

The submarine was *U-755* of the 29th Flotilla under the command of Walter Göing. He was appointed to the newly commissioned boat, *U-755*, and promoted to Kapitänleutnant on 1 January 1942.

When news of the Hudson sighting was received, Göing must have decided to fight it out; if he was thinking that the twin-engined American-built aircraft carried only four depth-charges and he could afford to risk them, he was wrong. It must have come as a nasty surprise when he eventually found out the new attacking weapon that it carried. The guns on the U-boat were hurriedly manned, and as the Hudson circled to attack from the port quarter, the pilot saw grey puffs coming from the light anti-aircraft fire.

When the aircraft was down to 850 feet, some eight hundred yards from the U-boat, the first salvo of rocket-projectiles were released at a twenty degree angle to the sea. One of the salvo failed to release but the other was a direct hit on the waterline beneath the conning-tower. In the second salvo four more rockets were fired from 660 yards astern of the conning-tower, this time all the rockets released, but the first one entered the water eighty feet short although two others hit amidships of the conning-tower under the water and another less than ten feet astern of the conning-tower. No visual damage was seen but the submarine started to go round in circles thirty seconds after the attack as if out of control and two sets of flame and a small amount of smoke appeared just aft of the conning-tower hatch.

The submarine then almost stopped and started to settle with decks, aft the conning-tower, awash. Bubbles were seen as if tanks were being blown to keep the U-boat afloat. No wreckage or oil were observed but large air bubbles and foam were seen each side of the conning-tower. The Hudson circled the U-boat four times, on the third time round the crew were seen to be diving overboard with others leaving the conning-tower in a panic. The aircraft dived and attacked the crew with the front turret guns. Soon afterwards the bow of the U-boat lifted half out of the water and it sank stern first, nine minutes after the attack. When the aircraft left for base, forty of the crew were counted in the water.

Arriving back at Blida just after 1530, Flying-Officer Ogilvie reported the success of the new weapon, and that the submarine had kept up a continual fire on his Hudson until it began to settle; no damage or casualties were experienced. The front guns of the Hudson were found to have fired over a thousand rounds and a further 6,000–7,000 rounds were fired from the turret.

While the 608 Squadron commander was sending a report on the success of the rocket-projectiles to Coastal Command headquarters, Spanish warships were rescuing some of the crew of the U-boat. Nine men, all wounded, were landed at Valencia. Walter Göing, the commander, was not amongst them.

A week later, on 4 June, Hudson F-Freddie of No 48 Squadron sank *U-594* at the western approaches to the Mediterranean and this was the final victim of the Hudsons based in and around Gibraltar.

XVI

Desert Squadron

At the eastern end of the Mediterranean No 459 RAAF Squadron was formed using RAF serialled Hudsons. The formation of this squadron was forecast by Headquarters RAF Middle East in August 1941, the intention being that it should be composed mainly of Australian personnel and be attached to No 201 Naval Co-operation Group as a naval co-operation unit. The reasons for the creation of No 459 Squadron and for its Australian identity were explained when it actually came into being in February 1942, by Air Vice-Marshal L. H. Slatter, Air Officer Commanding No 201 Naval Co-operation Group. He wrote:

> To meet the growing air requirements over the Eastern Mediterranean, Air Ministry authorised an expansion of No 201 Naval Co-operation Group last year. This expansion took the initial form of providing more reconnaissance units; and to this end, No 459 Squadron was formed. With the view that there was always a possibility that Australia might some day be faced with a similar problem around her coasts, it was further decided to man the unit entirely with RAAF personnel, thus providing Australia with a reserve of her own personnel trained in G.R. work.

It was decided that the squadron should be provided with sixteen Hudson aircraft as initial equipment, but in the meantime, war came to the Far East and the machines intended for No 459 Squadron were diverted there. It began its career, therefore, with the sum total of two Hudsons and four Blenheims some forty miles west of Alexandria, at Burg-el-Arab, on 10 February 1942.

Based on the fringe of the Western Desert, with its unenviable reputation as one of the dustiest spots in that dusty region, the nucleus of the squadron operated from LG05 at Sidi Barrani under the control of No 235 Wing. From there on 14 February Squadron Leader P. Howson and Flight Lieutenant I. L. Campbell, 'B' Flight leader, in the two original Hudsons, made the first two operational flights. The CO's trip was uneventful, but Campbell, with whom Wing Commander Johnson, commanding officer of No 203 Squadron, was flying as navigator to familiarise himself with the performance of Hudson aircraft, had some excitement and some bad luck.

First, a Malta-bound convoy was sighted and photographed. It consisted of three cruisers, one anti-aircraft cruiser, fifteen destroyers and three other vessels, shadowed by a Ju88 from 5,000 feet. Then, an hour and a quarter later, the feather wake of a submarine periscope was sighted from 1,500 feet. Diving from a thousand feet the Hudson released a stick of four bombs, two of which failed to explode. Both live bombs fell beyond the target, ten and fifty yards away, respectively.

The work of building up a complete squadron continued slowly. By the end of March the strength was eight officers and 129 airmen. Then, to assume command, Squadron Leader K. S. Hennock arrived on 19 April. On the ground the squadron was assuming shape but aircraft were slow in arriving and in March and April the only operations were two flights from Egypt to Malta, the Hudsons setting a course which was followed by Hurricane reinforcements for that hard pressed island. May, however, saw the welcome arrival of seven more Hudsons, bringing the total strength to nine. In the middle of that month a move was made to LG40 at Behig, five miles east of Burg-el-Arab.

It was also in this month that two Welshmen, Richard Roberts and Gerry Spring arrived at Port Tewfik in Egypt to join the squadron after a two month voyage from England round the Cape. It is Taffy Roberts who recalls:

Practice bombing was carried out but one morning in June enemy tanks were seen on the distant hills so the squadron moved to LGZ, Gineifa. 59 patrols were flown during June and then we started on offensive sweeps against tankers carrying fuel for the Afrika Korps. In the middle of June Tobruk fell and the next month Rommel was at El Alamein.

It was about this time that General Wavell had some near misses while flying in a Hudson. His aircraft taxied to the runway through a blinding sandstorm when one of its wheel brakes seized up – this was repaired and the General climbed back aboard. After being airborne only fifteen minutes the oil pressure gauge on one engine dropped to zero and the pilot had no option but to return to the landing strip. By the time the dust had been cleared from the filter the sun was setting. The General took off once more but after twenty minutes the oil gauge fell back and the pilot tried to carry out the, dangerous task of flying on only one engine. Within a short time this engine began overheating and the pilot had no option but to make a forced landing. He managed his aircraft skilfully but one brake seized up and the Hudson took a wild swing, tipped over and ripped off the port wing and the greater part of the tail.

Richard Roberts, a fitter, was allocated to N-Nuts, the commanding officer's Hudson. He says the Burg-el-Arab runway was the usual desert strip, flat, dusty and covered with small stones. The camp 'entrance' consisted of two 40-gallon oil drums painted white. One day some of the Aussies while down for a bathe found a sea-mine, loaded it on to a lorry and had just reached the camp entrance when it exploded; there was no lorry, no camp entrance and no men after the explosion.

Now, in the middle of summer the squadron life went on from day to day in the midst of a terrific heat wave. Ground crews worked in aircraft at a temperature of 125 degrees. Air raid alarms came and passed, and at this time the squadron was given its most dangerous and difficult job. Rommel and his Axis hordes were held by the Eighth Army at El Alamein, but Tobruk was in the enemy's hands and from here he was bringing supplies down the coast to Sollum and Mersa Matruh. These supplies were transported in barges, known as 'F' boats, and were well capable of taking care of themselves. Of welded steel, they had a length of 156 feet, a beam of 21 feet, and a draught of $3\frac{1}{2}$ feet and displaced about 320 tons at approximately eight knots. Their main armament consisted of 3 inch anti-aircraft guns mounted near the superstructure at the rear. Machine-gun fire was experienced, particularly from the bows and starboard side. Almost always all fire was intense and accurate. The 3 inch ack-ack was effective and accurate up to about 1,000 yards with the aircraft right at sea level, and the Bofor type, which was sometimes experienced, up to about 700 yards.

This, then, was the opposition which the attacking aircraft had to expect. Each of the barges was said to carry the equivalent of ninety or more fully-laden trucks. The disruption of this traffic was vital and the first attack, on 28 July, was made on two barges, one of which was afterwards found beached. Four Hudsons participated, escorted by seven Beaufighters. The first Hudson dropped its depth charges on the rear barge from mast-head height, but was hit by ack-ack, the port engine set on fire and the aircraft compelled to force-land in the sea where it sank, tail-first, in under two minutes. Another Hudson was hit at 40 feet and the pilot received a slight shrapnel wound in the right forearm. Another crew member was seriously wounded by shrapnel, an artery being severed, but the gunner acted with splendid promptitude and applied a tourniquet. The aircraft was considerably damaged, but despite this and his own wound the pilot made home and a perfect landing – the first barge attack had not lacked excitement but in all July was a bad month for casualties as six crews were lost.

Attacks were made almost daily for the first fortnight in August. The plan was to come upon the barges as soon after first light as possible, before they could be given fighter protection. In conformity with this policy, Flight-Lieutenant I. F. Rose, 'coming out of the grey mists of the dawn', as a newspaper subsequently described it, gained three direct hits from twenty feet on 2 August. Pilot Officer V. K. O'Brien did not get away scot free on 10 August, when he scored four or five direct hits in the midst of intense ack-ack. His port engine was hit and caught fire, the port wheel burst, the wings were sprayed and the aerials shot away. Flying on only one engine, the pilot found the greatest difficulty in gaining height. The belly gun and two side guns, with their ammunition, were thrown overboard, and still the aircraft would not gain height. Overboard went the flame floats, ASV equipment and all loose fittings, and the disabled Hudson limped home 250 miles to make a perfect landing.

These 'bombing the barges' attacks, as they were known by the pilots, cost the loss of four Hudsons during August, the Axis lost 13 fuel carrying vessels. September was to prove an eventful month. Detachments were sent to Palestine and Aden, being employed on escort and anti-submarine duties. On 4 September Pilot Officer Heaton attacked a destroyer at low level and left it ablaze. He was piloting one of seven Hudsons on a dawn shipping strike when the destroyer and two other vessels were sighted, he attacked the destroyer with ten 100 lb bombs from forty feet. As his aircraft flew through the ack-ack barrage there was a terrific explosion. The Hudson was hit in the starboard wing; both aileron cables were cut, and it was also hit on the starboard end of the tailplane. After circling to see the result of its attack, the destroyer was burning fiercely with dark smoke pouring from it, the aircraft headed for home, where it arrived after 6 hours 47 minutes in the air.

Four days later six crews were briefed for an attack on an enemy convoy north of Derna, but owing to an accident on take-off only five got away. Squadron Leader Campbell was practically airborne when a vicious flick developed, one undercarriage leg collapsed and the aircraft spun round on its wing tip and caught fire. All the crew made their escape before the bombs exploded. The take-off of the other aircraft was thus considerably delayed, with the result that only Pilot Officer Proctor found a target. Despite the fact that there could be no surprise he attacked a 5,000-ton vessel from 30 feet, scoring two hits. The ship listed to port and smoke poured from the stern. On 12 September the same pilot sighted a U-boat while on patrol from Palestine, but unfortunately for him all his depth charges hung up at the crucial moment, as the submarine crash-dived.

The long expected attack by the Eighth Army began in bright moonlight on the night of 23 October at El Alamein. For several hours a hell of fury was let loose on the enemy's positions before General Montgomery's army, well supported from the air and by artillery and tanks went forward on the attack. The Allied air forces working in perfect co-operation with the ground forces kept up a non-stop blitz on enemy troop concentrations, landing strips, transport and supply lines, well over a thousand sorties were carried out on the first day alone. This attack was the beginning of the long road which threw the Axis out of Egypt into Libya. On 13 November the Eighth Army continued the swift pursuit of the fleeing enemy forces across Cyrenaica and reoccupied Tobruk and Gazala. The air attacks continued without any opposition from the Luftwaffe which had been beaten out of the skies before the Battle of Egypt had opened. One of the heaviest attacks in the Western desert was made on the docks at Benghazi before its occupation by British and Dominion troops on 20 November.

In the meantime, at the other end of the Mediterranean, the first parties of the American Expeditionary Force had been put ashore at many points on the coasts of Algeria and Morocco early on 8 November, in 'Operation Torch' already mentioned.

No 459 Squadron moved forward from LGZ Gineifa, near the

Great Bitter Lakes, to Gianaclis in the wine-growing area on 28 November and then later on to Gambut, the ground crews having a night stop at Giza. At Gineifa Sergeant 'Dinger' Bell's tent had caught fire and burnt out, his service revolver, hung up on the tent pole, blasted off shots as it got hot!

This service revolver was required again shortly as during their stay in Egypt No 459 Squadron had acquired some pigs. When the time came to move camp the problem of how to transport the pigs, which were not officially on the squadron's strength, arose. The problem was solved by tying them in sacks, fixing them to the bomb racks, then closing the bomb doors. Hence it was probably the Hudson that flew the first 'pigs in space'. On arrival at Gambut the bomb doors were opened and the pigs tumbled out to be herded into a ten foot square hole two feet deep which had been surrounded with 40 gallon fuel drums on the side covered and banked up with earth. The pigs were fed on cookhouse swill, and, being in an Aussie squadron, the pigs fed well, being especially fattened for Christmas. When the day for the slaughter came a shear leg was put up, another square hole was dug and filled with a tarpaulin to hold boiling water. The Sergeant cook then enticed the first pig to one side and hit it square on the head with a 7 lb sledge hammer, *Bonk*. The pig shook its head, decided this was not a very friendly act, jumped the 40-gallon drums and made for the enemy lines! Squadron members set off in hot pursuit when they saw their Christmas dinner escaping and this time a timely shot from a service revolver brought home the bacon.

The quick moves meant in fact that the squadron enjoyed three 'Christmas' dinners that year as the storekeepers did not want the trouble of transporting vast quantities of food from one camp to another so it was eaten before the moves.

All of No 459 Squadron arrived at Gambut on 18 December. Gerry Spring recalls:

While the squadron was moving from Egypt to Gambut after two or three days we arrived at Sollum Pass. This is a series of sharp bends up the escarpment, one lorry at a time went up or down. The gharries came to a halt as coming down the pass was a gharry with wogs, chanting and wailing, escorting the blanket covered bodies of Eighth Army soldiers who had been killed in the battle, on their way to a Christian burial ground. The eerie wailing echoing down the pass created a macabre atmosphere that will be remembered for ever by the squadron members.

The winter rains of 1942/3 flooded the camp area at Gambut and afterwards multitudinous flowers and shrubs appeared very quickly and some were quite pretty. In retrospect it is the good things that remain in the memory but the thought of sitting in a tent, gazing out across the sodden sand, through the steady rain to other dismal-looking tents and a Hudson looking so forlorn that it appears as if its wings are drooping, shivering at the same time, are difficult to erase from the back of the mind. Indeed, weather conditions were often extremely unfavourable, but it was a rare exception for an aircraft not to complete a patrol as briefed. Half the sorties necessitated night take-offs or landings – sometimes both – from strange airfields. Night patrols now predominated. As one pilot said on posting: 'Now I will have to take a conversion from night to day flying!'

A typical one of these night sorties is remembered by squadron flyer R. Williams:

'It is night, a dark still night with a slight chill in the air. Overhead a canopy of stars form a domed roof for the airfield.

'A torch flashes, voices are heard in an indistinct murmur. Several figures emerge from a dark shape that is a tent and cluster around the darker shape of a gharry. A match flares as someone can enjoy a smoke even at this ungodly hour of 0230. Two doors slam, a starter whirrs and the engine settles into a quiet purr as if afraid to intrude on the quiteness of this Egyptian night. "All aboard?" murmurs the driver. "Yeah! Take her away," is the laconic answer from the back. The note of the engine rises and the darkness is diffused a little by shrouded headlamps. The truck moves off, out on to the airfield. Soon it is among the bigger and darker shapes of the kites.

'The crews climb down and disperse to their different Hudsons. Doors are opened, cabin lights switched on, covers ripped off and windows wiped over. Props are turned with much grunting and a few muttered curses. Four men clad in flying kit, lugging chutes, harness, dinghy packs and helmets climb into each machine after a last lingering drag at a cigarette. Doors slam and after a few moments of indistinct movement a head appears at the pilot's window, faintly silhouetted by the dash panel light. "All clear port?" is the question. "All clear port – contact" is the promptly-given answer. A high pitched whine, cut short by the shattering roar tells of engines that have been well looked after and tuned to perfection. First one and then the other, and finally all the kites are adding their share to the bedlam of noise. Dust rises in clouds behind the machines, hanging still in the night air and forming gritty choking clouds that make the black shapes outlined by red, green, and white lights all the more blurry and hard to distinguish. Motors roar, scream and die down to a murmur as switches are tested.

'Then from the long line of white lights which form the flare path a beam of green light flashes at the first machine, – the OK from the Control Pilot. Number one moves off, awkwardly to outward appearance, but somehow giving the impression of immense power that seems to reflect the determination of the men inside. A last check-up at the end of the flare path, then the motors roar into a unified howl and the machine moves forward slowly at first but with ever increasing speed until finally she is off and can only be identified by a white light slowly moving upwards in the dark sky. One by one the machines take-off until all is quiet again. The little group of men standing around the truck are left behind. "Oh well, let's go back to bed", is the unanimous opinion, and once again it is, "All aboard. OK let's go", and the truck moves off.

'Once more the airfield is quiet, a silence undisturbed, while somewhere in the star-spangled immensity of the night a handful of men are sitting in different aircraft in different positions over the water, shrouded in darkness, watching for their targets, their prey that is so vital to the Hun.

'Just one night in many nights, but nights that will never be forgotten by those who know.'

It is at times like these, as the writer so rightly recorded, that the ground-crews should be remembered as their gharry is speeding them back across the airfield for a doze until their charges return. During one of these breaks Leading Aircraftman Bedser composed a poem to the aero-fitter.

> He wears a suit of faded blue,
> No brévet on his chest,
> And you'll find more streaks of castor oil
> Than medals on his breast.

He wields a hefty spanner and a bit of oily rag
While the other fellow shoots the Hun
And boasts about his bag
He works in mud and slush and rain
And curses the bloody war,
And wonders ninety times a day
What he joined the Air Force for.
He's just an aero fitter nothing more and nothing less
A suit of greasy overalls in place of battle dress
But he strikes a blow at the dirty Hun
With his honest British skill
As sure as the airman who aims the bomb
Or gunner who makes the kill.
And when you've handed out the DFM, and DFC and such,
Just think of the aero fitter,
Who does not ask for much;
Shake him by the hand and smile,
Knowing he did a lot
To make those roaring aeros safe
For the man who fires the shot.

Aero fitter Gerry Spring says: 'The ground staff went on occasional flips, which were really test flights, and this low level flying was enjoyed as a distraction from the monotonous daily routine.'

His fellow Welshman, Richard Roberts, also went on one of these flights:

> Most of our flying was at sea level, 20 feet high. I flew on detachment from Gambut to St Jean, fifteen miles north of Haifa, at sea level. While at St Jean an armourer de-bombing a Hudson of depth charges was killed when one of the depth charges blew up, we spent the afternoon picking up pieces of him, made up the weight with sand bags and buried the poor lad with the usual rifle drill and ceremonial. We flew back to Heliopolis, our major overhaul base, and then to Gambut again at sea level. There were three Hudsons in a tight V-formation. We flew from the sea over the low coastal strip, then up the side of the escarpment, low over the camp at Gambut, then up into a bomb burst of the Prince of Wales Feathers, and we were home.

As mentioned earlier, heavy falls of rain made conditions in the camp unpleasant and mud was almost as frequently seen on the seats of pants as on boots. On dark and rainy nights slit trenches often harboured aircrew fumbling and slipping towards the operations tent for briefing.

The Aden detachment returned at the end of the year, but not before two crashes had occurred; taking off from Socctra in the early morning, a Hudson bounced into the air before gaining flying speed, touched a wing tip and crash-landed. The crew and passengers were unhurt except for the navigator whose leg had to be amputated subsequently. Despite his grave injury he crawled through a hole in the fuselage and beat out a fire which had started on the wing, over which petrol was pouring.

The Western Desert turned on one of the best specimens of its famous dust storms to mark the beginning of 1943 and for twenty-four hours sand and profanity filled the air. January operations were on a smaller scale than since the squadron first became really operative in June.

Life had its humorous moments. On 10 January the 'First Annual Western Desert Victory Dog Show', to give it its grandiloquent title, was a notable success. There were eleven classes – some for 'dogs' and some for 'general dogs' – and entries from several neighbouring units were accepted. The championship trophy was fashioned by armourers from an old shell case. On the eve of the show a 'Fighting French' general called to apologise for not being able to be present, at the same time entering his representative in the class for bitches with litter. The look on the Padre's face when informed that his 'Fleety' had romped home with a first prize for 'Bitch on Heat' had to be seen to be believed.

Most of the February sorties were routine convoy escorts along the coast; the weather was frequently bad and on one occasion aircraft flew in a full gale, with heavy rain. March weather was also abnormal. Rain fell in downpours and gales were frequent. For days the airfield was waterlogged and unserviceable. Patrols were frequently carried out in gales of unusual intensity, but only on two occasions were they cut short because of the weather.

While at Gambut the Hudsons were mainly used on anti-U-boat patrols carrying depth-charges which were loaded or unloaded so often by the ground staff that they became as familiar to them as the engines they worked on. The charges should only have detonated

RAAF ambulance aircraft in North Africa.

This Hudson photographed in the Middle East has USAAF stars and RAF fin stripes.

under water pressure so they were left around the camp in groups, but as Gerry Spring recalls:

> It happened one day returning to the flight from the fuel dump with a full bowser of petrol to refuel the kites, we saw billows of smoke rising from five or six depth-charges on the side of the path. We stopped the tanker saw that no one was in attendance but when someone shouted: 'It's OK they will burn out as they will not fire, only under-water pressure'. We continued on our way and had got about 30 yards away in the full bowser when there was a terrific explosion – the depth-charges having detonated; so much for the water theory – or was it the rain? No harm came to us but an innocent member walking in the camp received a piece of metal in his leg and required treatment in the sick bay.

Richard Roberts went on leave to Alexandria and on arrival back at camp found that his charge, N-Nuts, was pranged upside down, the story being that some pilots – not the commanding officer – used to warm up the Cyclone engines by running them on weak mixture giving what was called 'false cylinder head temperatures'. When they tried to take off, the engines being really cold, the kite would drop out of the sky. Gerry Spring saw the incident, he says it was a tragic event. The Hudson took off just before daybreak and the engine cut out, resulting in the Hudson crashing upside down. The pilot was decapitated and the rest of the crew were critically injured. The medical officer did a good job with the injured within his limited means on the desert camp. Later they were flown to Heliopolis in a specially adapted Hudson in order to avoid the long journey over execrable roads to the nearest hospital but unfortunately another subsequently died. Gerry Spring says that Hudson prangs usually ended in burn-ups, but there was not one in this case.

A successful inter-unit sports meeting of quite an international character was held in the middle of March, with British, Australian and American competitors. The Americans had been coached by a former Olympic Games winner and included several athletes of more than local prominence in their own country, and they scooped the pool. The sporting spirit displayed in the competitions was of the best and nobody grudged the Americans the cup, presented by Wing Commander Howson.

The flooding of the camp in the middle of March coincided providentially with the opening of the new officers' mess, built on slightly higher ground, with a concrete floor. It proved waterproof and windproof so the sergeants, whose own mess was under water to a depth of several inches, messed with the officers. The rain continued, almost the entire camp was under water and the airfield was unserviceable.

Despite these handicaps the squadron's aircraft serviceability figures that month established another record at 90.5 per cent. In April they rose yet higher to 96 per cent despite the heavy rain which seemed to single out Gambut for successive deluges, rendering necessary the operation of a detachment from El Aden.

The amount of shipping in the squadron's patrol area increased still more and aircraft escorts increased accordingly. On 19 April a U-boat was sighted 40 feet below the surface on a course which would allow it to intercept a convoy. As the U-boat was only visible when the aircraft was directly overhead a successful attack could not be made, but a smoke float and depth charge were dropped to mark its position and destroyers commenced the hunt.

April also marked the stage when some of the long-serving aircrew became tour expired and were sent as instructors to pass on the benefit of their experience to new recruits at flying schools. It was only right that those who had borne the heat of battle and survived should be rested, but for most of them instructional duties were not welcome, there was not the same camaraderie as that within a front-line squadron as one of those posted at this time recorded:

'My first feeling of resentment at becoming a so-and-so instructor type is now tempered by the reflection that it had to come sooner or later anyway. But although my stay with the squadron has been a little less than twelve months they have been quite eventful months and a host of memories and faces flood my mind.

'First, at dusty fly-infested Burg-el-Arab, greeted warmly by the solitary Pommy in the officers' mess and equally warmly by the Aussies who were to prove such good cobbers. A little later quite strong English reinforcements were able to match Westminster Abbey against Sydney Bridge, Piccadilly with King's Cross and Worthington's Bitter with Ballarat.

'Then a quick move to Gineifa, landing on its barren spaces, sleeping underneath the aircraft, waiting for the road convoy to

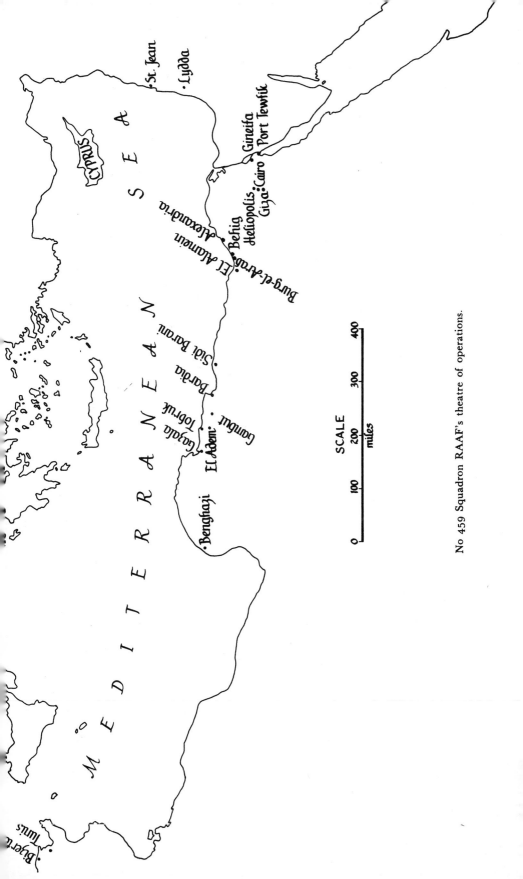

CYPRUS

St. Jean   Lydda

Gineifa   Port Tewfik

Heliopolis   Cairo

Giza

Befig

Burg-el-Arab   Alexandria

El Alamein

MEDITERRANEAN   SEA

Sidi Barani

Bardia

Sollum

Tobruk

Gazala

El Adem

Benghazi

Bizerta Tunis

SCALE

0   100   200   300   400

miles

No 459 Squadron RAAF's theatre of operations.

wend its weary way to us, watching the line of vehicles file in twenty-four hours later with a specially interested eye for the cookhouse. Then in an incredibly short time the camp springing up around us, showing how Australians have the happy knack of making themselves comfortable in the shortest time.

'Next time when we moved we missed the faces of many who would never accompany us again, victims of the grim detachments on strikes. But we remember them . . . we remember still and always.

'We remember the confidence with which we entered an aircraft before a trip, relying on the proved efficiency of our conscientious ground staff. We had only the enemy to contend with. We remember a host of little incidents, some humorous, such as when Arthur Newton, 2,000 feet above the sea, sneezed his teeth out through the cockpit window. They are probably auxiliary molars to some proud fish now. We remember Wing Commander Hennock listening with ear glued to the radio to the dulcet tone of "Lili Marlene". We remember Lofty Stanwell and others becoming blood brothers and earning the proud title of "Digger" by judicious use of the Doc's scalpel. We remember 'A' Flight slogan issued by Squadron Leader Campbell from which it appeared that a certain degree of hotness was not hot enough.

'And so with the recollection of some of the lighter moments we say farewell to No 459 Squadron, happy at the thought of lasting friendships forged in the desert, not to be broken by time and distance.'

Their replacements arrived in the form of twenty-five new personnel from the United Kingdom and 75 direct from OTU's. The majority of these were comparatively untrained operationally, so an intensive programme of lectures and training flights was started.

As the veteran flyers went home the war continued to the west. At dawn on 6 May the British First Army, supported by masses of bombers and fighter bombers, launched the final offensive for Tunis from the south. On the following afternoon advanced elements of the army entered Tunis. Meanwhile, in the north the American and French troops, who began their offensive at precisely the same time as the First Army, were making equally rapid progress to Bizerta. An American force, led by the Second US Corps, poured into Bizerta in the afternoon of 7 May.

Richard Roberts continues:

From Gambut we used to go to Tobruk for food and Bardia for water. At Bardia we cleared out some bombed buildings and stayed the night, swam all day and night, and returned to camp the following morning for Squadron Bath Day. On one occasion the Aussies stuffed shells and other pyrotechnics into a road mending machine – the ones that used to look like Stevenson's Rocket – put a 3-inch shell into the fire-box door and shot at the cap from a safe distance. When one of the shots hit the cap the machine blew up with an almighty bang. On another trip to Bardia some of the Aussies found a Cyclone engine rolling up the shallow beach and dragged it out and took it back to Gambut. The Engineering Officer at Gambut was a Polish Jew who we knew as Mr Joseph; he used to ride a BMW hell for leather all over the desert; he identified the engine as one from the squadron by its engine number and plate. The sea had given up one of a crashed Hudson's engine.

It was mentioned earlier that Richard Roberts went on leave to Alexandria. Other members of the squadron spent a day in Tobruk, the small coastal town in Cyrenaica that had played such a vital part in the struggle for Egypt, one recorded his impressions at the time :

'It was with a feeling that I was trespassing on hallowed ground that today I drove down the road into Tobruk.

'As I looked down on the town I felt that nowhere could one find a more peaceful scene. The sun's warmth was reflected in the blue water of the bay and I felt the urge to go down and dive into the calm, inviting water. On the other side of the harbour the white buildings stood out against the brilliant blue of the sea. Even at this distance I could distinguish the graceful arches and columns which betoken an Italian town. The harbour was full of ships, as befitted a prosperous Mediterranean port.

'But these impressions of serenity were shattered as we drove around the harbour and into the town. Once proud ships had their decks awash, others were burnt out and bore mute testimony to the effectiveness of bombing – twisted tangled metal. In the middle of the harbour lay a ship with its decks awash; others were burnt out and bore still water. I looked at the liner down by the stern and thought of gay parties on board when it plied perhaps between

Naples and New York. And what of Mussolini's delicate architecture? Here was ample evidence that Heinkels, Hudsons, Wellingtons and Liberators had passed this way – not a square foot of the white walls left unscarred by shrapnel, buildings blown to pieces by direct hits, and here and there strong columns severely shaken by near misses. From a vantage point we silently contemplated the scene of nature's beauty on the one hand and man's destruction on the other, and my companion said "The BBC was right – 'A graveyard of Mussolini's hopes and ships!' "

'Higher up on the hill we came to the church. As we entered we removed our caps, feeling that though the roof is gone and only the shell remains, it is still a church – a place dedicated to God. We looked at the angel, still standing at the altar though scarred by bombs; at the names of Australians, Englishmen and Italians scribbled on the Lectern. On the front steps we looked back, was it the skill of Italian craftsmen who made beauty rise above the ruins or was it something deeper – God's presence still being felt in the devastation that is Tobruk?

'The next hour I shall remember as one of the anachronisms of war. We drove to a green spot, spread a tarpaulin on the grass, set out our bread, butter and tin of sheep's tongue, with tomato juice for refreshment, and, as we ate, talked of other picnics back home in Australia, laughed as we promised to tell the story of a picnic lunch at Tobruk to our ain folk after the war, and earned the surprised scrutiny of soldiers passing by.

'As we sat there in quiet peace I began to think of Tobruk in different mood, of Churchill's words "The Empire garrison will hold Tobruk" of how those brave men of the Second Australian Infantry Force, the British troops and the little ships of the Navy had proved to an Empire grown wary of good news that their leader's words were no idle boast. I thought of how the RAF and later the Americans had more recently borne the brunt of its ack-ack barrage and of the airmen who had sunk the Axis ships before they could reach the doubtful safety of its harbour and the protection of its guns. But today, thanks to the all conquering Eighth Army, the RAF and the Navy, Tobruk is ours, as the Luftwaffe learned a few nights ago when they sent six Ju88's to bomb it. Four of them came to earth in flames. I wonder how many times the Tobruk garrison has cheered that same spectacle?

'On the hills and in the wadis as we drove away we saw the

trenches, caves and barricades of stones. Our thoughts were of the men of the 2/13th, 2/43rd and the other famous battalions, and we remembered – the Rats of Tobruk.'

There was still a war being waged elsewhere in the Mediterranean, night bombers attacked enemy bases in Sicily and Italy as the war was taking a turn for the better for the Allies. May 1943 is now generally recognised by historians as the turning point in the war; all organised resistance in Tunisia ceased and 291,000 Axis prisoners were taken, the Germans lost 41 U-boats and the Ruhr dams were breached.

It was about this time that Gerry Spring recalls an ENSA party visited the camp at Gambut :

After the show a kite en route to Heliopolis for major overhaul was used to take the party back to Cairo. After take off the pilot shot up the camp at tent height but when he tried to pull the kite up it did not immediately respond and we watched it come closer and closer until very slowly there was some response to the stick. The damage had already been done and the tents were blown from their stakes but the ENSA performers were none the wiser to their near mishap.

Gerry Spring, although a ground crew man was involved in some near-misses himself :

I went on a test flip in a Hudson flown by the 'A' Flight Commander and after normal tests we shot up the drome. Near the officers mess was the signals tent, which had a long thin pole sticking up; I was standing in the astro dome midships watching the stunt as we came in low, the pilot obviously did not see the aerial and we hit it, it whiplashed and a large hole appeared in the starboard wing, so large that I could see daylight through it.

Later we moved to a temporary strip in Palestine and then we were sent on to Ramat David. The first aircraft to fly in was full of fitters and riggers. The commanding officer was already waiting for us at the end of the runway. We made a good landing and were rolling on, then a commotion up front indicated that the brakes had failed. Now, Hudsons were renowned to go up in smoke on impact, and one Aussie rigger did not wait for the event but wrenched open the door, lowered himself out, and ran like hell with his legs going like pistons. He shot out at an angle and luckily the tail plane missed him. The commanding officer was standing blissfully unaware of the drama about him, he watched the Hudson come on, then the pilot swung the aircraft round on engine power encircling the watcher before finally coming to a stop. There were sighs of relief all round except from the rigger who bailed out; he was still out of breath at the evening meal.

As mentioned earlier detachments of No 459 Squadron had moved to other bases in the Eastern Mediterranean and all detachments celebrated the squadron's birthday on 1 June. The anniversary of the beginning of operations in real earnest, it heralded what was to be one of the most successful months in No 459 Squadron's history. A record number of hours was flown, there were three submarine sightings and from one of these came the first kill.

At base the birthday itself was celebrated by a squadron dinner, which coincided providentially with the arrival of beer.

On 16 June Flight Sergeant Dave Barnard and his crew took off from Lydda in their Hudson, T-Tommy, at 1220. Its task was to co-operate with naval vessels in a hunt for a U-boat which had previously torpedoed a tanker in the Haifa area. The naval vessels were not met in the position given, so Barnard climbed to 3,000 feet to take advantage of cloud, and commenced an independent search. No doubt the lectures he had been given in the technique of attacks came flooding to his mind when two hours later a U-boat was sighted on the surface four miles away.

Under normal conditions, it was decided, the pilot should go straight for his objective from whatever direction presented itself and waste no time in jockeying for position. There were occasions, however, as in this instance, when a pilot could stalk his prey from behind cloud cover, and in such cases the question arose as to what method to choose. There was no doubt that with depth charges an attack along the track from astern offered the greatest chance of success.

In the first place, by approaching from directly astern, the pilot had the wake and swirl to give him his line of approach and by making full use of this, line error was eliminated. There was a clear field of fire from the front turret not only to the U-boat's AA gun but also on the conning-tower hatch, so that a determined front gunner was able to prevent any return fire. Finally, if the stick was correctly placed it was possible to get all weapons within lethal range.

The main aim was to catch the U-boat on the surface or nearly there. Nothing had to be allowed to compromise this, for from whatever angle the attack was made, it had to get home.

The pilot and navigator of T-Tommy were both trained in Australia and the others in Canada. The crew had flown together with Coastal Command in England and Ireland and were new to the Middle East. It was only their third operation with No 459 Squadron. So the Hudson crew relatively inexperienced in Mediterranean conditions were pitted against a U-boat flushed with recent success. On 12 June, *U-97* torpedoed the small Dutch steamer *Palima* and three days later, the day before it was attacked sunk the British 9,000 ton tanker *Athel Monarch*.

The U-boat had left its base at Pola on 5 June under the command of 27-year-old Kapitänleutnant Hans-Georg Trox, who was not to survive the attack.

The crew of *U-97*, a Type VIIC boat launched at Kiel nearly three years earlier, could not have been keeping a good look-out for when the Hudson was a matter of a few hundred yards away, the pilot and navigator could see the Germans on deck stripped to the waist enjoying the sun. It was probably only then that they heard the sound of the aircraft's engines above their own diesels. The sunbathers scrambled for the conning-tower but as the pilot said afterwards, 'I had 200 yards to go and 200 mph on the clock. It wasn't a race.'

The captain released his depth-charges at less than 50 feet up the track. Two were near misses and a third was a 'dry hit'. The submarine immediately circled hard to port, and members of the crew dived overboard. The blast from the explosion of the direct hit blew the Hudson up 400 feet and the pilot temporarily lost control. All control surfaces were damaged by the blast; the wing tips had curled up causing the ailerons to jam and the pilot said, 'You could put your head through the holes in the elevator and tailplane. All windows and escape hatches had caved in and the interior of the aircraft was a shambles.'

Shorty Purcell, the rear gunner, thought he was going to join the Germans in the sea when the force of the explosion lifted him and his turret a foot out of the aircraft. George Crisp was bombarded by his navigational gear and finished up nursing the compass which was wrenched from its bracket and tossed into his lap. Brian Cobcroft found himself flat out on the floor of the aircraft underneath a couple of pans of ammunition.

Despite the severe damage to the aircraft, the pilot stayed on the scene for half-an-hour, long enough to see most of the remaining crew members jump into the sea before the U-boat made its last dive stern first with its bows high in the air.

Equally as meritorious as the classic surprise attack on *U-97* was the skill with which Dave Barnard succeeded in flying his now unstable aircraft safely back to base where, according to his crew, he made the best landing he had ever made. The damaged wireless had been useless on the return trip. The Navy picked by 21 survivors. None of the aircraft crew was injured.

'A classic example of a perfect submarine attack,' commented No 201 Headquarters and this not only reflected credit on the crew, but was a tribute to the training in Empire Air Training Schools, and on the squadron for the few weeks preceding the commencement of their operations in a new sphere under different conditions from those encountered by the crew in the Atlantic. It also emphasised the value of surprise brought about by good hunting methods in a well-camouflaged aircraft, followed by immediate action, resulting in a certain kill. The Navy signalled: 'Many thanks'. Flight-Sergeant D. T. Barnard from Melbourne received an immediate award of the Distinguished Flying Medal.

There was a tremendous party held that evening to celebrate Dave Barnard's success and there were a few sore heads the next morning.

At the end of the month the Air Officer Commanding No 201 Naval Co-operation Group wrote:

Once again No 459 Squadron is to be congratulated on its effort, not only for this month, but also for the quarter. In view of the large amount of night flying carried out by the squadron, theirs is a really fine record which should be the aim of all other units.

In July the squadron carried on with their patrols but the U-boats must have retreated westwards to cover the Allied landings on Sicily; *U-97* remained the sole sinking by the squadron, despite many hours of tedious flying in all types of weather.

In August Air Chief Marshal Sir Arthur Tedder visited those airmen still remaining at Gambut, his son had served with No 459 Squadron. August also heralded one of the greatest air raids of the war when the US 15th Air Force finally extinguished the oilfields at Ploesti. On 3 September the Italian mainland was invaded, and then followed the Aegean campaign in which the squadron undertook night bombing operations against German airfields in support of the British landings on the islands of Kos and Leros as well as shipping in the area.

On the night of 20/21 September 459 Squadron raided Kalamaki airfield at Athens with 13 Hudsons while Heraklion was raided with another five Hudsons. At this stage of the war the Hudson was reaching the veteran stage, and, as in other operational areas, it was replaced, in No 459 Squadron's case by the larger Ventura from the same stable. The worn out Hudsons were flown back to the United Kingdom, and it is probably these that ATA pilot Lettice Curtis wrote about :

A source of trouble on the Hudson was the de-icing boots on the wing leading edge. In early 1944 the Air Transport Auxiliary were called in to collect a Hudson from Holmsley South in the New Forest, which had been flown in from the Middle East and had been landed, one must suppose, at the first airfield in England that came into view. The task fell to one of the senior members of the headquarters staff, who had only recently completed his Hudson conversion course. Nobody at Holmsley South had ever seen a Hudson but eventually, the crew satisfied themselves as to the serviceability of the aircraft and made their departure.

The runway at Holmsley South was a long one, but even so the Hudson with full engine power refused to become airborne and the take off ended in an adjacent field minus wheels and engines, and with what was left of the aircraft catching fire. The pilot and his flight engineer were lucky indeed to escape.

In due course the ATA Accidents Committee decided in their wisdom that the pilot was to blame for having allowed the aircraft to become airborne without adequate flying speed. During the next few months three Hudsons were lost in similar accidents, in each case the crew being killed. It was at this stage that Coastal Command put in hand an investigation which showed that all four Hudsons had recently returned from the Middle East where they

Loading bombs into a Hudson on New Year's Eve 1942.

had been parked out in the tropical sun. The sun and heat, it was decided, had split the rubber of the wing leading edge de-icing boots causing a breakdown of the air-flow over the wings. After this the rubber was replaced by metal sheeting.

Meanwhile No 459 Squadron served out the rest of the war in the Mediterranean area attacking towns and shipping, with Baltimores eventually replacing the Venturas.

Rubbing the sweat from our foreheads and shaking the dust from our eyebrows I think we will end this Middle East sojourn by showing the spirit of the time, and the thinking of the time with the Australians in the desert as summed up in a poem written by Don

Baird that appeared in the first edition of *Gremloid*, the squadron magazine, in April 1943.

You're round the bend my son – IF

If you can find your tent when all around you
Are howling winds and stinging flying dust,
If you can eat your bully beef and biscuits
And show no sign of your heartfelt disgust,
If you can bear to hear those mournful statements
'Beer's rationed' or worse still 'No beer'
And say 'Mahleesh' 'Lime juice and water'
And drink it down with every show of cheer

If you can dare to give the wogs your dhobi
And get it back again each week – complete
And never lose a handkerchief or towel,
Then smile benignly upon the thunder seat
If you can cheerfully climb aboard a gharry
And bounce and bump across the landing ground
And never mutter curses on the driver,
Or if you do – don't mutter them too loud.

If you can sit still at night and play at poker
And gamble with your next fortnight's felooss
And tho' you're losing keep on betting madly
And pay your debts all round with I.O.U.'s,
If you can take your share in drinking sessions
And find your own way back to bed at nights
And rise again next morning bright and early
And shaved and washed report at 9 to flights.

If you don't mind the smell that comes from butter,
If you're mahleesh about woggy bread
If you can reach the mess in time for breakfast
And never, never want to stay in bed,
If you can really hope to reach Australia
Before this war is well and truly done,
You're just a bloody marvel brother!
And, what is more, you're round the bend my son!

An aerial view of the wartime Tempsford airfield at Gibraltar farm in rural Bedfordshire. On close inspection both Halifax and Hudson aircraft can be seen at dispersal.

XVII

Resistance Rendezvous

Before the war Tempsford was a little known village just off the A1 in rural Bedfordshire. From March 1942 its airfield at Gibraltar Farm housed aircraft which transferred agents and saboteurs to occupied Europe and the single-engined Lysanders and twin-engined Hudsons landed in France under the very noses of the Germans. During the three years, until the end of the war, Nos 138 and 161 'Special Duties' Squadrons which occupied the airfield transported over a thousand agents, 10,000 packages and 29,000 containers to Western Europe.

No 138 Squadron had been reformed in 1941 and No 161 was formed at Tempsford in 1942. This latter squadron took on the main task of landing in enemy held territory.

In October 1942 Wing-Commander P. C. Pickard was appointed in command of No 161 Squadron. Charles Pickard, a pre-war regular airman, had become well-known to the British public as Captain of F-Freddie in the propaganda film 'Target for Tonight'. This story of a Wellington raid on Germany filled the cinemas in early wartime Britain. The blond six-foot-four pipe-smoking Yorkshireman epitomised the 'press-on' type of airman.

In February 1942, while with No 51 Squadron, Pickard led the squadron's Whitley's which flew paratroops across the Channel to wreck the German radio location unit at Bruneval.

Although still only 26 years old Pickard had completed two operational tours, fought over Dunkirk and had spent fourteen hours in the cold North Sea awaiting rescue, when he crash landed his Wellington which had received anti-aircraft shell damage in a raid over the Ruhr.

Up until the time the newly appointed Wing Commander arrived the twin-engined Whitley aircraft carried out long-range parachute drops and the smaller Lysander made clandestine landings in France.

Once settled in Pickard quickly learned the role of the Special Duties aircrew and flew on operations himself. Now, well experi-

enced, at the turn of the year the new Commanding Officer sought
a twin-engined aircraft that could land in France; the Lysander was
only suitable for carrying a small load over a short distance. It was
considered that it would be possible for a Hudson to perform a pick-
up operation from enemy occupied zones. Wing Commander Pickard
led his pilots in the training for this particular work and it was
found that the Hudson needed a clearing of 1,600 metres by 800
metres to be able to land and take off again.

The trials with the Hudsons proved successful and the first Hudson
operation took place on the night of 25/26 November. A code
sentence, meaningless in itself and only understood by the listening
French agents, was transmitted on the BBC's European wavelength
at 1930 and all preparations should have been made. The Hudson
left the Bedfordshire airfield just after eight in the evening, its
destination Avignon in the South of France. On arrival at the spot
the pilot could see no lights on the ground, and no sign of any runway. The pilot did see some flashes but he carried out his instructions and returned without landing in France, for the flashes may
well have been made by Germans who had heard of the expected
arrival and hoped to capture the Hudson and its invaluable agents.

Charles Pickard carried out his most interesting Hudson rendezvous
on the night of 24/25 February 1943. He took off at 2227 and
crossed the French coast just before midnight. The destination was
Tournus on the Saône, almost on the Swiss border. Over France
Pickard had to fly by dead reckoning as fog prevented any sightings.
The fog persisted as far as Le Creusot where the weather cleared,
but later there was fog in the target area which was reached at 0130.

While the Hudson was flying blindly over France, the reception
committee below had their own problems. Since they had notified
London of the precise point on the Michelin map for the pilot to
land, the Germans had strewn the field with mounds of bricks.
When the code phrase had arrived the previous evening they had all
turned to, moved the bricks and attempted to level out the field.
While the Hudson circled above, the work below became more frantic
as the bricks were dispersed. Eventually the landing torches were
lit but owing to the fog and the position of the field the landing
was extremely difficult and about twenty attempts were made before
the aircraft finally came in to land. The Hudson descended in a long
sweep, lower and lower, and with undercarriage down it approached
the ground. Pickard could never had been prepared for what was

to happen next. As the Hudson landed on the ground, a tremendous splash went up as the wheels touched, throwing up mud, like waves. The pilot kept his head, and the aircraft level, as he squelched his way to the end of the run, which was on firmer ground. He turned the Hudson ready for a quick take-off into the wind. The outgoing agents quickly alighted and the returning personnel took their place; it was carried out in two minutes.

Pickard opened the throttles but the aircraft refused to move. It was stuck in the mud. He released the brakes and tried again but still the Hudson refused to budge. Quickly the door opened and the passengers jumped out. They, with the new arrivals positioned themselves round the wheels and the wings. Pickard accelerated and they all pushed but still the aircraft held firm. Pickard cut the engines, opened the cockpit door and, in French, asked who was in charge of the reception committee. When the leader was forthcoming, he received a blast from the peeved pilot who said :

'You've nothing to be proud of, not only have you landed me in the backyard of a brick factory, but in the centre of a bog into the bargain.'

'We knew the RAF could land anywhere' said the leader.

'Land maybe,' replied the pilot, 'but I'll be damned if I know how we shall ever take off. Besides, your flare-path stinks, just have a look at those trees. They're not 1,500 metres away. I'll never clear them with this load. You get your chaps to fix me a new one running diagonally across the field and then, if the gods are willing, I might just manage to clear that corner over there !'

The passengers and torch bearers set to work with a will and this new task took them over an hour. At anytime now the Germans might arrive; they must surely have heard the Hudson circling and clearing its engines after it landed. The fear of their arrival was sufficient incentive for the working party to go all out. In the meantime Pickard and his crew were supervising the layout of the new flare-path.

Pickard finally entered the cockpit on his own, for the crew were going to help with the pushing. The engines singly came to life, then Pickard from his higher vantage point saw a farm-hand leading two horses. He despatched one of the reception committees to bring them to aid the take-off. They were quickly secured ahead of each other and harnessed to a strong upright beside one of the wheels by a length of chain. Pickard started the engines, the pulling of the

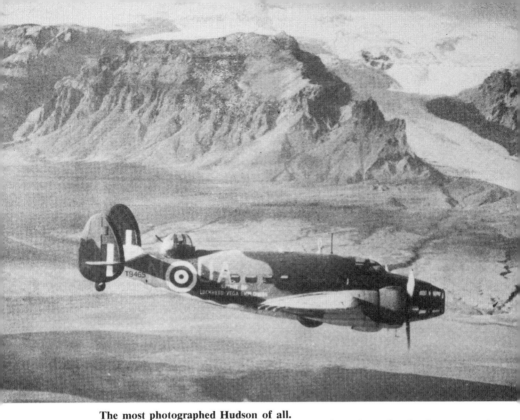

The most photographed Hudson of all.
The inscription 'Spirit of Lockheed Vega employees' can be clearly seen on the side of the aircraft as it flies over glaciers. . . .

from the Coastal Command airfield at Kaldadarnes. . . .

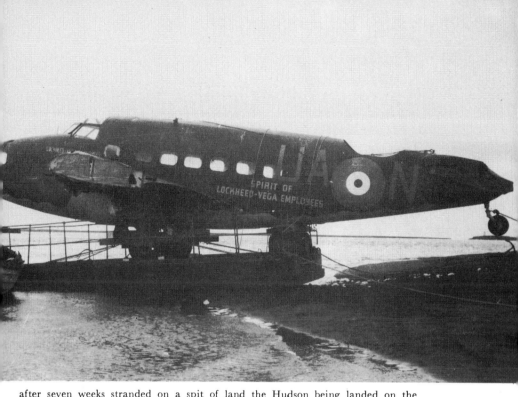

after seven weeks stranded on a spit of land the Hudson being landed on the barge. . . .

to transport it to a ship so that it could receive proper workshop attention when landed.

frightened horses and the pushing of the panting men was sufficient to move the aircraft on to drier ground. The horses were released, the Hudson took up its new position into the wind, the passengers embarked, the flare path torches were lit, the engines were brought to life and the aircraft shuddered while near full power was applied. Then the Hudson was off, flames shooting from the exhausts, the bricks were avoided as it sped across the field; it had reached over half-way before it became airborne and it was still low as it approached the trees at the end of the field. The Hudson rose at the very last moment and in doing so clipped one of the trees. Those on the ground heard the snapping of a branch mingled with the noise of the aircraft's engines. The wing-tip and the leading edge were broken off one wing and the undercarriage was jammed in the down position, but worst of all for Pickard, 'George' the automatic pilot, was put out of action. It was 0530 when the Hudson took off and set course for home. Flying low across France and out through Normandy, crossing the coast near Le Havre ninety minutes later, Pickard thought his luck had held long enough and wirelessed for fighter assistance back to base. None was forthcoming but the Hudson landed safely at base an hour later with a very relieved pilot, crew and passengers. For his adventures on this night Wing Commander Pickard earned a bar to his DSO.

The 'Moon Squadron' Hudsons could only land if the moon was right, and it was two months before Pickard flew one again to France. This was just a routine trip on the night of 15/16 April. The Hudson took off from Tempsford at 2208, landed its two passengers and twelve suitcases in France at 0100 and took off fifteen minutes later with eight returning passengers and their luggage. There was some disappointment for three intending escapees, but eleven passengers arrived for the return flight whereas only four had been expected. The Hudson arrived back at base at 0325, after a text book operation.

Pickard undertook his last Hudson operation two nights later on 18/19 April. His Hudson took off at 2155 for France with two hundred pounds of luggage. The weather was excellent with good visibility and no cloud, nevertheless, some difficulty was experienced pin-pointing the actual landing ground. However, the aircraft landed at 0215, spent twenty minutes on the ground discharging its cargo, and, embarking eight passengers took off and reached base at 0415, with no light of dawn to assist the landing.

On 5 May 1943 Wing Commander P. C. Pickard, much against his wishes, was finally grounded after completing over 100 sorties. He left the squadron, and on promotion to Group Captain, took over the station at Lissett in Yorkshire.

The following month the most photographed of all Hudsons, 'The Spirit of Lockheed Vega' joined 161 Squadron. As mentioned earlier in the book, this aircraft was built by the employees of Lockheed and Vega in their spare time, with materials supplied by the firm and presented to the people of Britain at Christmas 1940. The Hudson, a Mark III, took off from the works in Burbank California on 22 December and arrived in Montreal on Christmas Day from where it was flown to England by Captain Donald Bennett, as leader of the fourth and last, of the group flights to Britain arriving on the 29th – just a week after leaving the factory. On the way over from Newfoundland there was a radio failure which prevented communication with the other aircraft during the flight.

With the inscription 'Spirit of Lockheed Vega Employees' painted along the side of the aircraft, and just below the cockpit, the Hudson soon caught the imagination of the British press.

On 3 May 1941 the Hudson joined No 269 Squadron of Coastal Command and later in the year went with them to Iceland for anti-submarine duties out of Kaldadarnes. After carrying out these duties successfuly for a year, the Hudson was forced to make a crash landing in bad weather. The landing was made on a narrow spit of land without serious damage to the machine. Later a crew set out from the mainland to salvage the aircraft, an operation which owing to the impossibility of bringing cranes and heavy haulage gear, had to be done slowly and laboriously by hand. Extreme weather conditions made their difficulties greater and seven weeks and two days had passed before the operation was finally completed. The Hudson later went to a civil repair organisation before joining No 22 Maintenance Unit. At the beginning of June 1943 'Spirit of Lockheed Vega Employees' joined No 161 Squadron at Tempsford.

The first operational sortie was carried out over a month later on the night of 16/17 July, by Group Captain 'Mouse' Fielden. The aircraft took off at 2250 from the advanced base at Tangmere, for a point near Tournon in south-eastern France. Fielden was due to land two agents and sundry packages for the French Resistance, but was unable to make any contact with the ground. After trying in vain for some time to see signs of activity below, it became obvious

Wing Commander P. C. Pickard introduces the Secretary for Air, Sir Archibald Sinclair, to his crew fallen in under the shadows of their Hudsons in April 1943. P/O McCairns was a Lysander pilot and F/O Broadley was the Wing Commander's navigator and was with him when they were killed in a Mosquito after the Amiens prison raid with their new squadron.

to the pilot that due to the lack of darkness it would be better for him to carry on to North Africa than risk returning across heavily defended Northern France at dawn. Accordingly he carried on to Maison Blanche in Algeria, landing at 0635. Fielden reported in, then settled down for some sleep before the return journey.

One of the Maison Blanche pilots took up a Bristol Bisley for a test flight as it had been fitted with a new engine. Inconceivably the new engine fell out of the Bisley while in flight. The pilot was able to bring the aircraft back to the airfield on the remaining engine where he landed, just avoiding two parked Halifaxes, but he then bounced hitting the visiting Hudson some six feet in from the tailplane. Several people were injured, not least the pilot.

Group Captain Fielden was justifiably annoyed at losing his famous Hudson after the first operational flight in its new squadron's colours through no fault of his, and had to return to Britain as a passenger in a Lancaster that had also used the airfield for a diversionary landing. Another passenger on the Lancaster was the pilot of the crashed Bisley returning to England for hospital treatment. It was recorded in No 161 Squadron's diary that the Hudson was lost through another aircraft 'landing on it', and the 'Spirit of Lockheed Vega Employees', T9465, was officially written-off on 21 July 1943.

Moving on to 1944, February again proved a bad month for Hudson landings. Just a year after Wing Commander Pickard's adventurous landing in France, another Hudson, piloted by Flying Officer Jack Affleek, who had joined the squadron just as Pickard was leaving, also had a sticky time.

The sortie was code named 'Operation Bludgeon' and took place on the night of 8/9 February 1944. After taking off from Tempsford at 2115 the target was located and a successful landing made at 2330 hours. The aircraft became bogged down whilst taxing back to the take off point and the engines had to be stopped. The pilot requested assistance and the aircraft was manhandled into the wind. The engines were again started but it was impossible for the wheels to get any grip and the tail-wheel sank into the ground. Now the main landing wheels sank to the hubs and the engines were switched off.

The reception party rounded up some villagers with a dozen oxen and six horses – yes, horses again. The beasts were hitched to the aircraft in an attempt to drag it forward out of the mud, but all to no avail. The pilot decided to dig channels in front of the wheels and try to taxi out on the engines, but time was now getting short and it crossed the pilot's mind that he might have to destroy the aircraft to stop it falling into German hands. When the digging was completed the aircraft was pushed clear and an attempt then made to take straight off but it was unsuccessful as it was impossible to get enough forward speed, so the motors were throttled back. While taxing back to the take-off point the Hudson again became temporarily bogged but this time it was soon cleared and at 0205 a final attempt was made to take off. This was successful, but only due to the skill and determination of the pilot. The aircraft hit a bump in the field when very near to the boundary and bounced and bounded into the air at 50 knots and managed to keep airborne.

Later in the month a woman agent recorded her thoughts about her flight. Taken by car to the waiting Hudson she alighted under the wing and thought the Hudson looked compact, and friendly. She found very little room sitting on the hard, cold metal floor which trembled as the engines roared into life. Inside the Hudson it became colder and colder and the agent was startled to hear machine-gun fire, but it was only the gunners clearing their guns over the channel. This agent was due to parachute from the aircraft and was pleased when the despatcher passed over a thermos flask containing hot tea at regular intervals until the dropping zone was reached. For this particular agent there was to be an anti-climax as no signal was received from the ground and she was returned to Britain until she successfully landed during the next month.

Of the aircraft flown by the pilots of Nos 138 and 161 Squadrons, only Lysanders and Hudsons regularly landed in France, but now the invasion of Europe was about to begin, the Hudsons broadened their field of operations.

Originally many of the crews of No 161 Squadron were Polish, but inevitably they became tour-expired. In March 1944 eight new crews joined the Hudson flight from Coastal Command, but this work of landing in occupied territory was not everybody's cup of tea and two pilots who were found unsuitable for the work had to be replaced.

After the invasion in June, and when the Allies had secured a secure foothold in Europe, the Hudsons from the squadron were required as transport aircraft as well as continuing their assistance to the Resistance. In October agents were dropped in Holland, and Hudsons were ferrying in supplies to France and Belgium.

One of the Hudsons that failed to return. This picture was taken by the Germans off the coast of Holland – the aircraft has never been identified with certainty but it could possibly be aircraft R-Rodger from No 161 Squadron that took off at 0150 on 6 July 1944 with four crew, four agents, three packages and ten pigeons and was never heard of again.

In January 1945 a new wing commander took over the squadron, transferring over from No 138 Squadron. At the end of the following month he took part in an operation to check up on the work; unfortunately his aircraft failed to return, so a new commander was again required. In all, during the month of February, there were twenty Hudson sorties of which over half were successful, and a total of 22 agents were dropped in Denmark and Germany.

In the following month, the Hudsons widened their scope yet again when an operation was carried out in Norway. There were seven successful sorties during March and these mainly consisted of dropping agents into Germany. Unfortunately there was a heavy price to pay, as by now the Hudson had reached the veteran stage and the Germans were finding it increasingly easier to shoot them down. On the night of 20/21 March, Hudsons L-Lucy, N-Nuts and

O-Orange set out for Germany and all failed to return. This was indeed a shattering blow. It later transpired that the latter two had been shot down on their way out as a result of enemy action. The pilot of N-Nuts had a miraculous escape when his machine was attacked and hit by a night fighter; two explosions occurred in mid-air. The pilot was thrown clear as the Hudson disintegrated. He found himself falling through space but had the presence of mind to pull his parachute rip-cord and made a safe, if heavy, landing. He was eventually found in a dazed condition and badly burned about the face and hands, but his wounds were not serious and he was returned to hospital in England.

The last wartime Hudson operation of No 161 Squadron took place on 24 April. On this occasion two agents were dropped over Mindelheim in Germany at 0200, then the aircraft went on to drop leaflets in the Steinham/Memmingen area. It was about this time that Mitchell aircraft were due to take over from the Hudsons of the squadron, but the end of the war at the beginning of May put a stop to this move.

With the end of the war the Hudson pilots had the pleasant task of flying home released prisoners-of-war, mainly from Brussels. The very last casualty of the squadron happened during one of these mercy missions. On 18 May the pilot of Hudson L-Lucy took off for Lüneburg, where the surrender had been signed, to assist in the transport of former prisoners. It appears that there were insufficient British prisoners to make up a full load and so the pilot was given a load for Brussels. He reached Evere and made a normal approach and touched down. However, he bounced badly and took off again, while flying level he suddenly climbed steeply, fell back in a tail slide, stalled and nose dived to the ground where the aircraft burst into flames. There were no survivors.

The following day another Hudson took off for Brussels to investigate the cause of the crash and identify the victims. A further three days later another Hudson flew to Brussels so the crew could attend the funeral of their colleagues. Both Hudsons brought back returning prisoners-of-war. These were the very last Hudson missions as No 161 Squadron was disbanded on 5 June 1945.

Altogether the Hudsons carried out 39 pick-up sorties, of which 33 were successful and no aircraft was lost; 143 full Hudson operations were carried out, half of which were successful and only ten aircraft were lost. This operational record is very impressive, especially when it is remembered that the flying casualties include losses in England.

There are still many of the Lockheed models preserved to remind us of the great work achieved by the *ATTACKER – the Hudson and its flyers.*

The Grand Duchy of Luxemburg honours the Hudson crew of N-Nuts No 161 Squadron; as reported in the text the pilot escaped. The Hudson engine marks the grave of an agent, probably of the Belgian Army.

Additional Reading

In chapter XVII the account of Wing Commander P. C. Pickard's landing on a brick-strewn field was first published in *Duel of Wits* (Hodder & Stoughton) and is published with permission. Its author, Peter Churchill, was a British agent working with the French Resistance. The book is one of a trilogy on this work written by him.

Wings of Night, the secret missions of Group Captain Charles Pickard, DSO and two bars, DFC (William Kimber & Co 1977) is the biography of the famous airman. It was written by Alexander Hamilton whom I met in London when he visited this country. For further stories of Nos 138/161 'Special Duties' Squadrons see my book *Raider – the Halifax and its flyers* (William Kimber & Co Ltd).

Lettice Curtis gave permission to be quoted in two chapters. Her book *Forgotten Pilots* (G. T. Foulis & Co) deals with the interesting activities of the Air Transport Auxiliary and their important contribution in the 1939–1945 conflict.

For further reading of the wartime service of *Nordmark*, attacked by Hudsons in 1940, see my book *Under Three Flags*. The voyages of *U-331*, attacked by Hudsons a year after sinking HMS *Barham*, and the life of the man o'war, can be read in my *Battleship Barham*. Both publications by William Kimber & Co Ltd.

Lockheed Hudson Marks I to VI by Christopher F. Shores is No 253 in the Profile Aircraft series.

Phonetics

In this book I have been inconsistent in calling aircraft by different names, at the same time there is a reason for this. Take the case of the commander of No 459 RAAF Squadron who flew N-Nuts, if he used the official phonetic he would have flown N-Nan, hardly an inspiring aircraft name in which to lead a squadron into battle.

It must be remembered that phonetics were used to distinguish the initial letters in transmission rather than as aircraft names. The phonetics were changed more than once during the war, especially so after the Americans entered the conflict. The list below is that which prevailed in mid-1943:

A-Able	N-Nan
B-Baker	O-Orane
C-Charlie	P-Peter
D-Dog	Q-Queenie
E-Easy	R-Rodger
F-Fox	S-Sugar
G-George	T-Tare
H-How	U-Uncle
I-Item	V-Victor
J-Jig	W-William
K-King	X-X-ray
L-Love	Y-Yoke
M-Mike	Z-Zebra

Glossary of Abbreviations and Terms

AMC	Armed Merchant Cruiser
A/S	Anti-submarine
ASI	Air Speed Indicator
ASV	Air to Surface Vessel (Radar)
ATA	Air Transport Auxiliary
ATC	Air Training Corps
Desert Rats	7th Armoured Division, their insignia was a jerboa (desert rat) (also known as 'Rats of Tobruk')
E & RFTS	Elementary and Reserve Flying Training School
ENSA	Entertainments National Services Association (colloquially 'every night something awful')
Felooss	Money
Gharry	Egyptian carriage, hence any vehicle in Egypt
HSL	High Speed Launch
L.G.	Landing Ground
Mahleesh	Indifferent, 'couldn't care less'
MTB	Motor Torpedo Boat
NCO	Non Commissioned Officer
OTU	Operational Training Unit
RDNAS	Royal Dutch Naval Air Service
St Elmo's Fire	Ball of light sometimes seen on ships masts and aircraft wing tips during storm
u/s	Unserviceable (colloquially 'useless')
USAAF	United States Army Air Force

U-Boats lost to Germans through Hudson attacks

Date	U-boat Nr.	Cause of Loss	Position
28. 8.41	570	Hudson S No 269 Squadron RAF	N. Atlantic
1. 3.42	656	Hudson P-8 No 82 Squadron US Navy	Off Newfoundland
15. 3.42	503	Hudson P-9 No 82 Squadron US Navy	S.E. of Newfoundland
1. 5.42	573	Hudson M, No 233 Squadron RAF	W. Mediterranean
7. 7.42	701	Hudson No 369 Squadron US Army	Atlantic Coast U.S.
31. 7.42	754	Hudson of No 113 Squadron RCAF	Off Nova Scotia
30.10.42	658	Hudson Y, No 145 Squadron RCAF	E. of Newfoundland
30.10.42	582	Hudson N, No 269 Squadron RAF	N. Atlantic
14.11.42	595	Hudsons F, L, K. W & X, No 500 Squadron RAF	W. Mediterranean
15.11.42	259	Hudson S, No 500 Squadron RAF	Off Algiers
17.11.42	331	Hudsons of 500 Squadron and Albacores from H.M.S. Formidable	W. Mediterranean
19.11.42	98	Hudson C, No 608 Squadron RAF	W. approach to Med.
12 2.43	442	Hudson F, No 48 Squadron RAF	Off Portugal
4. 3.43	83	Hudson V, No 500 Squadron RAF	W. Mediterranean
28. 3.43	77	Hudsons L & V No 48 Sqn and L No 233 Sqn RAF	W. Mediterranean
5. 4.43	167	Hudsons W & L No 233 Squadron RAF	Canary Islands

Date	U-boat Nr.	Cause of Loss	Position
7. 5.43	447	Hudson X No 233 Squadron RAF	W. approach to Med.
17. 5.43	646	Hudson J No 269 Squadron RAF	W. of Faeroes
19. 5.43	273	Hudson M No 269 Squadron RAF	N. Atlantic
28. 5.43	755	Hudson M No 608 Squadron RAF	W. Mediterranean
4. 6.43	594	Hudson F No 48 Squadron RAF	W. approach to Med.
16. 6.43	97	Hudson T No 459 Squadron RAAF	E. Mediterranean
17. 8.43	403	Hudson O No 200 Squadron RAF and French Wellington HZ No 697 Squadron RAF	Off Dakar
5.10.43	389	Hudson F No 269 Squadron RAF	N. Atlantic

Squadrons operating Hudsons

RAF Squadrons :   24, 48, 53, 59, 62, 117, 138, 161, 163, 194,
                       200, 206, 217, 220, 224, 233, 251, 267, 269,
                       320 (RDNAS), 353, 357, 407 (RCAF), 459
                       (RAAF), 500, 608.
RAAF Squadrons :   1, 2, 6, 7, 8, 13, 14, 23, 24, 25, 32, 38.
RCAF Squadrons :   11, 13, 119, 120, 145, 442, 443.
RNZAF Squadrons :   1, 2, 3, 4, 9, 40, 41.

Abbreviated technical data of the Lockheed Hudson (Mark I)

Dimensions :   Span 65ft 6ins; length, 44ft 4ins; height,
                    11ft 10½ins.
Weights :   Empty, 12,000lb; loaded, 17,500lb.
Performance :   Max. speed, 246mph. Climb 1,200 ft/min.
                    Endurance 6 hrs. Service ceiling 22,000ft.
Armament :   Fixed forward twin 0.303 guns, twin 0.303
                    guns in dorsal turret, and one 0.303 gun in
                    ventral position. Provision also for two 0.303
                    guns in beam positions. Bomb load, 750lb.

Marks I, II and IIIA (A-29) were powered with the Wright Cyclone
engine and Marks IV (A-28) and VI (A-28A) with Pratt and Witney
engines.

Index